Buying & Selling
Teddy Bears

by Terry & Doris Michaud

Portfolio Press

DEDICATION

We dedicate this book to the memory of the late Pam Hebbs, British teddy bear
expert and good friend. She will be greatly missed by many.

First edition/First printing

To purchase additional copies of this book, please contact:
Portfolio Press, 130 Wineow Street, Cumberland, MD 21502
877-737-1200

Library of Congress Control Number 00-131634
ISBN 0-942620-38-0

Project Editor: Krystyna Poray Goddu
Design & Production: Tammy S. Blank

Cover photo: Doris & Terry Michaud
Cover design: Kourtney Mills

Printed and bound in China

ACKNOWLEDGEMENTS

We wish to thank the following people for their valued assistance with facts, figures, contributions and moral support in our efforts to write this book: antiques & collectibles dealers and experts, including Dee Hockenberry, Mort & Evelyn Wood, Linda Mullins, Karen Strickland, Adrienne Zisser, Robert & Delores Buntz, and British dealer and expert Sue Pearson; collectors Peter & Joanne Krusche, Karen Silverstein, Don & Helene Marlowe, Judi Dolan, Jo Nell Harkrider, Marge Adolphson, Susan and Steve Swickard, and Kaye Mason; teddy bear artists Sue & Randall Foskey; show promoters Donna Harrison and Pat Moore; historian Peter Kalinke; and mohair expert Dr. C.J. Lupton; a great group of Canadian collectors, authors and, most importantly, good friends Donna McPherson (our liaison), Peggy Williams, Debbie Pontefract, Patricia Atchison, Evelyn Strahlendorf, Ken & Lynn Stanlake, Ruth Fraser, and museum curator Even Morton of the Tweed and Area Heritage Centre.

Last, a special thank you goes to the group that took our sometimes cryptic notes and writing and put it all together, the talented people at Portfolio Press, headed by editor Krystyna Poray Goddu. Without her talents and those of her staff, this book would not have been possible.

While we have made every effort to recognize and thank those who contributed to this book, names will undoubtedly come to mind long after it has gone to press. To those people, accept my apologies with the recognition that I was having a "senior moment" when the list was prepared.
                                                              —Terry & Doris Michaud

CONTENTS

INTRODUCTION

Teddy bear price guides are usually written by experts who have had many years of experience in the business, and have become familiar with various design factors that help them to identify certain manufacturers. More often than not, they deal in antique teddy bears—that is, they buy and resell teddies, know what the market conditions are and keep abreast of fluctuations by geographical region, by demand for a specific producer, and by other factors that affect the resale price. They are well suited to the task of producing a reasonably accurate guide to current values. Note we use the word "reasonably," as it is important to recognize that there really is no final authority on value. It boils down to an agreement between a buyer and a seller—nothing more, nothing less. We are frequently introduced as "experts" in this field, and my response to that introduction is that we will accept the title of expert if you accept the definition of an expert as somebody from out of town! I have seen many "experts" sharing their knowledge in the public arena, only to discover that they were in fact in error on a particular bear. I have been corrected on statements I have made, and rightly so, for none of us can be expected to know it all. We can only go by what we have learned over the years, and I consider it a lost day when I don't learn something new. With this in mind, recognize that, although we have made every effort to be as accurate in our descriptions as possible, there undoubtedly will be errors. We gladly accept constructive criticism and appreciate our readers sharing their expertise with us.

The reader should also bear in mind that the prices quoted represent our best assessment of the current market range for a given bear, and should not be considered as the final and absolute value. Prices vary greatly, depending on geographical location, current demand, condition, and a host of other factors. As a rule of thumb, prices do not go down on antique bears but can be expected to escalate in value through the years. Note that we said "as a rule of thumb," because there have been instances where certain teddy bears became very much in demand for a short period of time, until interest waned and values dropped.

The track record for collectible teddy bears is not as well established, and there is more of a price fluctuation for this group of teddies. By our definition, we consider teddy bears made prior to World War II to be antique, while those produced from the mid 1940s to the present time are in the collectible category.

Artist teddy bears present a whole new set of problems for establishing current secondary market value, as that market has not yet developed. Some artist-made teddies have increased in value on the secondary market, while others have not. We have attempted to address this situation in the section on artist bears. Because the secondary market for artist bears is totally unpredictable, most dealers suggest that collectors should never buy an artist bear on the basis of its future value but, rather, because they love it. If the bear increases in value, that is a bonus. When I am asked if a particular artist bear will increase in value, my response is usually: "It may do so, but probably not in my life time."

The intent of this price guide is not to establish values for antique or collectible teddy bears. It is to provide the reader with guidelines for price ranges for particular designs of a particular age. It is entirely possible that a reader may find similar bears listed in several guides under varying price ranges. This is unavoidable, due to the variety of factors (as outlined above) that affect a bear's value.

Finally, because there have been literally thousands of bear producers since the turn of the century, no single reference or price guide can hope to include them all. It may be difficult to find your exact teddy bear in a listing, as many bears through the years looked very similar. Indeed, it was not uncommon for some companies to copy the popular model of the day back in the early years. What's more, designers and bear makers often changed jobs, taking their experience, and even their patterns, to the next company. The best way to get a reasonably accurate value for a specific teddy bear is to have it appraised. While we ourselves do not, as a rule, appraise bears, our reference section (page 179) lists a number of companies and individuals who can provide this service.

IDENTIFYING OLDER TEDDY BEARS

When we cannot identify a teddy bear's maker, we can often date the bear by his materials—stuffing and outer coat. Most of the teddies commonly referred to as "antique" (made between 1903 and 1930) were stuffed with excelsior, also referred to as "wood wool." There are of course, exceptions and, in fact, many materials were used including sawdust, carpet remnants, and anything the maker could obtain at a low cost. Contrary to popular belief, straw was seldom used to stuff teddy bears.

In the 1920s some manufacturers discovered kapok, while others found the use of wool could reduce their costs because both materials were easier to stuff the bear with, reducing labor costs. Some manufacturers used a mixture of kapok and excelsior.

The fabric used for the earliest bears' outer coat (and for many of the collector bears made today) was usually mohair. It is an extremely durable natural fiber, but also costly. Later, in an effort to reduce their costs, manufacturers introduced a fabric referred to as art silk (an abbreviation for artificial silk), a man-made material that came into use in the mid 1930s. It did not have the soft feel of mohair and, as a result of buyer resistance, was removed from the marketplace after just a few years.

Cotton and wool, and some blends of wool and mohair, came into use for teddy bears in the 1920s and 1930s. Nylon blends came into use in the late 1940s, and the 1950s saw the introduction of another man-made fabric called Dralon. Today there are many man-made plush materials available, from very inexpensive plush used for craft projects to imitation-fur fabrics that have many of the characteristics of the real thing. Imitation furs of higher quality from Europe can be nearly as costly as mohair.

Traditionally, teddy bears were produced with shoe-button eyes; starting in the 1920s, blown-glass eyes on a wire stem were often used. This type of eye remained popular with manufacturers until the onset of child safety regulations after World War II, when the law required the use of a plastic safety eye attached more permanently. It would be reasonable to say that plastic eyes denote production after 1945, although the late 1930s and early 1940s saw the use of celluloid eyes (the forerunner of plastic).

There are many factors that make identifying antique and older bears so difficult. First of all there were literally hundreds, possibly even thousands, of companies and individuals producing teddy bears right from the earliest days. While Germany was, without a doubt, one of the largest centers for bear makers, other countries crafted their share as well. Steiff, with its famous metal button-in-ear, was one of the few companies that used some form of identification that could not be removed easily from their bears. Some makers used paper labels, while others used no labels at all.

Some producers made use of certain design characteristics, and knowing these can aid in identification. But we must be cautious about making blanket judgements about any particular characteristics, because often several companies may have used the same ones. For example, the German maker Petz is known to have used a small opening (or hole) in the head for inserting the ears. But we have seen examples of this in bears made by other companies as well.

Adding to the problem of identification, a lot of companies were quick to copy popular designs being produced by others. Steiff was (and is still) recognized as the most successful manufacturer of teddy bears for collectors, and there is no question that their designs were imitated. Early court records attest to Steiff going after firms that copied their designs, some of which also placed a metal "button" in the ears of their teddies. While Steiff was successful in stopping some of their imitators, other companies did manage to produce bears that had a striking resemblance to Steiff's more popular designs.

Many of the early bear companies flourished by maintaining a cottage-industry network of home workers, and indeed, some of the home workers produced teddy bears for more than one company. In the early days, Nuremberg was a center of teddy bear companies, with more than thirty manufacturers in that area of Germany alone. It was not uncommon for some of the employees, including designers, to change companies, taking their talents with them.

One country about which we have known very little when it comes

"Teddy," a Dominion bear from 1928, was acquired by the Tweed and Area Heritage Centre in Canada in 1991 after it was discovered tucked away in a trunk by the Meiklejohn family in Calgary. Teddy is 23 inches long with short mohair and stuffed with a mixture of kapok and excelsior. His head is triangular shaped, with large ears located on the side of the head. His foot pads are pointed at the tip, much in the same way the early Ideal bears were made.

to teddy bears is Canada. Recently Evelyn Strahlendorf, former editor of the *Canadian Doll Journal*, was kind enough to share some information she uncovered about one little-known Canadian company. The Dominion Toy Manufacturing Company was founded in 1911 in Toronto, Ontario, by Aaron Cohen, a former partner with Morris Michtom of the Ideal Toy Company in New York. Mr. Cohen was a sculptor and designer and had designed many of Ideal's character dolls. Dominion's first dolls were very likely made from the same molds as some of the first Ideal dolls. It is believed that Mr. Cohen may have been involved in the design of some of the earliest Ideal teddy bears. The first advertisements for Dominion bears in 1912 showed four different sizes of brown bears. They had a hump at the back of the neck, a long snout and long legs very much like the early Ideal teddy bears. Aaron Cohen left the Dominion Toy Manufacturing company after a few years, and his son Morris took over management responsibilities. The son changed his name to Cone and ran the company successfully until its closing in 1932. There are two excellent

The museum's other Dominion bear is from 1930. This 14-inch example has all of the same design characteristics as Teddy. Named Floyd, this bear is a more recent acquisition of the museum.

examples of early Dominion bears residing at the Tweed and Area Heritage Centre in Tweed, Ontario, Canada.

A Canadian bear also played a role in the development of an important British bear design. Teddy bears produced by Merrythought, one of Britain's oldest bear-making firms, have always had a special place in the hearts of Canadian children and collectors alike. One of the most popular bears by this British firm is a clever design called Cheeky, introduced at a British Trade Fair in 1956. The story goes that one of Britain's Royal family was visiting the exhibition, and upon seeing this new Merrythought design, is reported to have said: "My, he's a cheeky little fellow, isn't he?" Whether it is fact or fiction, it's a great story befitting a great bear.

But the story of Cheeky goes back to 1947, and has a direct link to Canada. The Merrythought bear that actually inspired the Cheeky design is a wild-haired, bright-eyed teddy called Punkinhead. Two great sources in Canada helped us put together the story of Cheeky and Punkinhead: Debbie Pontrefact, distributor for Merrythought in

Canada, and Patricia Atchison, editor and publisher of the *Canadian Teddy Bear News*.

Punkinhead was created exclusively for Eaton's Department Stores, specifically for their annual Christmas Parade. He was referred to as "Punkinhead, the sad little bear," and was instantly recognizable by the wild growth of hair that seems to go in all directions on his head. He was the hit of Christmas, and by 1948, Punkinhead merchandise of every description was offered. Merrythought was contracted to produce this lovable bear in plush form, and he continued to be a top seller for Eaton's for many years. Although his size, color and decoration changed from time to time, his unique topknot of wild, unruly mohair remained a constant. His popularity is not limited to Canada, as arctophiles around the world are pleased to add the stuffed mohair Punkinhead bear to their collections, particularly if they are one of the legions of fans of Punkinhead's successor Cheeky. Punkinhead is no longer produced, although a replica was offered in 1986, but Cheeky is high on the list of best sellers in the Merrythought family of designs and is sold worldwide.

In the end, don't be overly concerned if you cannot identify your beloved teddy bear. Experts agree that, by and large, the origin of a significant number of older teddies will remain a mystery. But then, very few people collect a bear because of its origin, but rather because it has that magic charm that tugs at the heart strings and says: "take me home!"

THE CARE AND FEEDING OF TEDDY BEARS

Once you have invested your hard-earned money in a teddy bear (or two... or three...) it's time to consider their care and feeding. We do not mean feeding in the literal sense, as everyone knows they are already stuffed! We use the term loosely to implant the thought that there are certain things that will need to be done to protect your investment.

MAINTENANCE

First let's consider maintenance of teddies that are new, or in prime condition, to start with. Since many teddies today are produced in mohair, we must be aware that this fabric is not only loved by bear collectors, but is also favored by moths, silverfish and other creatures that have been known to feast on it. It is therefore important to keep these bugs at bay. Moth balls can be used, but many of us are not fond of their smell. We found a suggestion in a helpful hints book that whole cloves are a deterrent for moths. We have used them for a number of years now, and have yet to find any moth damage to our bears, so we have to presume that it works. We simply pour a small amount into a paper cup and place the cups on the shelves by the bears. The cloves have a pleasant smell and may be a very good investment to deter moth damage. Some people use cedar chips in or near their bears; others choose potpourri as a deterrent.

If you have recently purchased an antique bear, you want to be certain that you are not bringing "bugs" or hidden larvae in with it. One of the best methods to eliminate that risk is to freeze the bear— literally! Wrap it in several layers of cloth and place it in a freezer for up to a week. This should kill any creatures that may have taken up residence inside the bear. After this "cryogenic" treatment, slowly bring the bear back to room temperature over a day or two.

Unless you have your bears sealed in glass domes, or protected from the atmosphere behind closed glass cabinets, it is necessary to give them a dusting on occasion. I have seen collectors simply shake a bear rapidly to free the dust, but most people use a vacuum cleaner to gently pull it out. Some even place a layer of cheesecloth over the end of the vacuum tube so as not to pull any mohair out, but if the bear is of more recent vintage that should not be necessary.

If you plan to store your bears, do not store them in plastic. This can lead to rapid deterioration due to condensation. You can wrap them in a cloth or plain paper and store them in a box. Do not use newspaper directly against the bear as the printing may rub off on the bear. A pillowcase makes a great storage container for bears of average size.

CLEANING

Is your newer teddy showing signs of needing a bath? If it is mohair it will clean up beautifully. Cleaning also helps eliminate the risk of moths and other creatures being attracted to dirt. Teddy can be surface-cleaned by the following method. First, get rid of any accumulated dust before cleaning. (Some detergents chemically react with dust to make a teddy bear turn green.) You can get the dust out by vacuuming the bear thoroughly, or by using an air hose to blow the dust out. I generally go to a gas station and use their air hose, holding it away from the surface of the bear to avoid damage from the strong air pressure. You can actually see the dust flow out in clouds.

Next, put some good wool detergent in a pan or sink and fill the basin with lukewarm water, making sure to create lots of suds. Fill a second pan or sink with clear warm water. Using a damp cloth (squeeze out the excess water) scoop up a handful of the suds and work it into teddy's plush in a small area, perhaps the size of the back. After you have worked it into the fabric and loosened the dirt, submerge a second cloth in the clear water, squeeze out the excess and wipe away the suds on the bear. Return to the suds with the first cloth and continue on a second area, wiping away the resulting dirt with the clear water cloth. Continue until teddy is done.

Place the bear on a wire rack or support that will allow air circulation all around, and let it dry naturally. Do not use a hair dryer or other similar means of drying, as this can damage the fabric. It will likely take overnight to dry, depending on conditions. Once the bear is dry, you can brush it out to restore that well-groomed look. Any stiff bristle brush should work well. We use a dog-grooming wire brush, which does a great job. If the bear is very old and you feel the mohair might be somewhat fragile, brush very gently.

REPAIR

Now that we have a nice clean bear, it's time to turn our attention to repairs that may be needed. Our rule of thumb regarding repair is to leave a bear as is unless it is a "life-threatening" situation. For example, if the pads are ripped open and the stuffing is falling out, this obviously needs attention. If there is a small hole in the pad it would be better to "seal" that area with a little clear-drying glue or fabric check to hold the stuffing in place rather than to replace the whole pad. A poor pad replacement may actually reduce the value of the bear. Pad replacement should be done by someone with enough experience to do it correctly. This procedure may entail removing the limb, removing the stuffing and turning the piece inside out to sew in the pad material as it was done originally. It also means using a replacement fabric that is as close to the original as possible. Some restoration specialists use antique fabrics and some dye a new fabric to match.

Simple repairs can generally be carried out by someone with limited experience, but if the bear in question is of great value and you want to maintain that value, look to a professional for restoration work. Simple repairs might include replacing a missing eye (in most cases, both eyes will need to be replaced in order to match) or re-sewing a loose ear. A skilled bear maker could also replace a missing floss nose and mouth, but in most cases, the remains of the original are better than a replacement.

Extensive repairs should be left in the hands of a professional restoration specialist. A question that frequently comes up is: "will repairing or restoring my bear hurt its value?" The answer is simple: if the bear has reached a stage where it requires repair, the value has already been diminished. Proper and professional restoration will recover all, or part of, that lost value. You will be amazed at the level of repair and restoration work that can be achieved today. Even with the extensive knowledge we have as a result of our doll hospital experience, we were surprised (and pleased) to learn that lost mohair can in fact be restored! In some cases it is done one hair at a time; in other cases, a section is replaced with a matching mohair fabric.

Since nearly all restoration work requires skilled labor, it may be expensive. A significant percentage of the work done in teddy clinics today is the repair and restoration of someone's first teddy bear, which has become a family heirloom. In such cases, price is not the prime consideration. But even in the case of acquired antique bears that need repair work, the cost of the repair is often more than recovered by returning the bear to a higher value. It has always been our contention that the condition of a teddy bear greatly impacts its value, so it is worthwhile to have the bear restored to as near its original condition as you can, and to keep it in good condition.

DRY ROT

Now let's deal with the most damaging condition in an old teddy bear—what is commonly referred to as dry rot. This term may not be technically correct, but it is widely accepted to mean the condition in which the fabric has lost most, or all, of its strength, and can literally split apart, even with gentle handling. To get a better understanding of the causes of this condition and to investigate potential solutions, we went to the Mohair Council of America and they, in turn, referred us to Dr. C.J. (Chris) Lupton, a professor in the department of Animal Science at Texas A&M University. Dr. Lupton works at the university's research station in San Angelo, Texas, and his area of expertise is wool, mohair and cashmere fiber production and metrology. He also has an extensive background working with cotton, so he was perfectly suited for aiding us in our investigation.

Dr. Lupton believes that the primary cause of dry rot is the cotton backing used in the production of mohair fabric. Cotton is much more susceptible to mildew attack than mohair. There are many kinds of mildew, and some cause the cotton to lose its strength. Other areas of concern pointed out by Dr. Lupton are: degradation caused by exposure to sunlight over extended periods; moisture (high humidity) that causes the cellulose in cotton to decompose; and an acidic atmosphere that can be found in some major populated areas.

In addition to our interview with Dr. Lupton, we also reviewed some guidelines for restoration and preservation of documentary papers and books from the Maine State Archives. As it turns out, some of the enemies of teddy bear fabric are also implicated in the degradation of important documents and papers. These include: atmospheric pollutants; sunlight and fluorescent light; mold and bacteria; and insects and rodents. The consensus reached by the Maine State Archives and Dr. Lupton is that paper products, and teddy bears, should never be stored in an attic, where temperatures can reach 150 degrees Fahrenheit in the summer. High humidity, often found in damp basements and some attics, can also create problems. We have always advised collectors to treat their bears as they would treat their children—don't keep them in the attic or basement!

If the dry rot is extensive there is little that can be done to reverse the deterioration process. If the dry rot has not advanced, however, Dr. Lupton suggests that coating the cotton backing with a type of latex like that used to protect carpets might prevent further deterioration. This treatment, however, would require complete disassembly of the bear in order to put on the coating. A product called Fray Check, often used by bear makers on the backing of the fabric to prevent fraying of the edges, might be helpful in slowing dry rot damage, as well. In the final analysis, the best means of avoiding the problem of dry rot is a careful examination of a teddy bear before purchase.

The proper care and feeding of your prized possession will pay off in many years of enjoyment for you and future generations to come.

Rating Antique & Collectible Teddy Bears

Technically, the word "antique" is only applied to items that are 100 years of age or older. Teddy bears, however, as we wrote in an earlier section, are generally considered antique if they were produced prior to World War II. Bears made after that time are considered "collectible" rather than antique.

One of the most abused areas in dealing with antique and collectible teddy bears is in rating their condition. Far too often a potential buyer is told that a bear is "in mint condition," only to have this phrase followed by a description that includes replaced pads, bald spots, color fading, etc. There is no question that the condition of the bear has a significant impact on its value, and this is probably the biggest reason for the tendency to overrate its condition. This section of the book is our attempt to establish some solid guidelines by which condition can be judged and to offer a value scale based on these definitions of condition. The value scale adds or subtracts points for each specific aspect of a bear's condition. By using this scale, we hope that readers will be better equipped to assign to their bears a more accurate value. First, then, we offer the following definitions.

MINT CONDITION

Also referred to as store stock, this is a bear that has never been played with, frequently has its original tags and is preferably in its original box. It has absolutely no signs of wear or use. Its condition is exactly as it was when it left the factory. Antique bears in this category are extremely rare.

GOOD CONDITION

This is the condition in which we all hope to find a bear. The bear shows some signs of "normal" use, but basically it has not suffered from play or age. It has minimal mohair loss (10% or less). It may have minor holes in the paw or foot pads, or professionally replaced pads, either in the original material or in a fabric appropriate to the era of the bear's production. It has no poorly done repairs.

FAIR CONDITION

A bear in fair condition shows some wear from play, and has some mohair loss (up to 30%). Color fading is minimal. Any missing parts (eyes or nose floss) have been replaced and any damage (torn or ripped fabric) has been repaired. It may have small holes in the paw or foot pads, but most of each pad is still intact. Some stuffing may be missing (10% or less).

POOR CONDITION

A bear in poor condition has excessive mohair loss (35% or more), excessive color fading and is often missing parts (ears, limbs, etc.). It is damaged from excessive play (mohair cut off, etc.). The pads are ripped open. More than 20% of the stuffing is missing. Any repairs to the bear have been poorly done. It may have a musty or smoky smell and dry rot, a condition in which the backing has become so fragile that it tears or splits under slight pressure.

There are certainly other conditions that we have not listed, and some of those listed can only be judged subjectively. It is our position that a bear in good condition achieves 100% of its listed value. Mint condition can add considerably more (50 to 100%) to a bear's value. A bear in fair condition should be in the range of 75% of its listed value, and one in poor condition should achieve approximately 25% of the value.

Since every teddy bear is a unique combination of the conditions described, we have developed the following value scale to assist readers in giving their bears a more accurate rating, and therefore a more accurate value. Following the scale, we show you how to use the scale on three bears in varying condition.

TEDDY BEAR VALUE SCALE BASED ON CONDITION

This system starts by assigning 100 points to a teddy bear that is in good condition.

Add Points for Each of the Following:

Never played with - all original (store stock) ....+25

Same as above plus original hang tags ....+25

Original undamaged box ....+50

Subtract Points for Each of the Following:

Eyes (one or both) missing or replaced ....- 5

Nose or mouth floss missing or replaced ....- 5

Small holes in pads (¼" or smaller on 18-24" bear) ....- 5

Stuffing missing (10% or less) ....- 5

Minor mohair loss (10% or less) ....- 5

Minor soiling ....- 5

Minimal color fading ....- 5

Smoky smell ....- 5

Ears (one or both) missing ....-10

Damage from excessive play (cut mohair, etc)...................-10

Large holes in pads or poorly recovered pads ....-10

Significant stuffing missing (more than 20%) ....-10

Excessive color fading ....-10

Excessive soiling..-10

Excessive mohair loss (35% or more)...............................-10

Musty smell ....-15

Dry rot (fabric splits easily) ....-50

If your bear has **125–200 points**, it is in **Mint Condition**.

If your bear has **85–120 points**, it is in **Good Condition**.

If your bear has **50–80 points**, it is in **Fair Condition**.

If your bear has **45 or less points** it is in **Poor Condition**.

By using this system, it becomes apparent that a teddy bear can have one major fault (large holes in paw pads, for example), but if all other conditions are positive, it can still have a good value. It should also be noted that many of these conditions can be corrected, but we highly recommend that most repair or restoration work be done professionally. (See our reference section beginning on page 179 for professional restoration sources). Professional repair work does not hurt the value of your bear, as the value has already diminished due to the work needed. Professional repair should return all, or most, of the lost value.

Because this value scale is somewhat subjective, it is only as good as the person using it. Therefore you must be honest and fair in applying the standards to ensure that you determine an accurate rating. Most price guides assume good condition when quoting prices. Our guide lists three price ranges (Good, Fair and Poor condition) for each bear.

To determine a price range for your bear using this system, first determine a price for the bear in good condition. Then determine the point rating based on condition. If the points total 90, then according to this system, your bear should be valued at 90% of the full value price. Since it is still in the Good Condition category with a 90 rating, you could even expect to get the full price.

Now let's look at some examples we can use to illustrate our system. Picture A shows a 22-inch M. Pintel-Fils French bear, circa 1948. It has very little mohair loss (a small spot on the back measuring 1½ inches long by 1/2 inch wide), so we subtract 5 points. The nose floss has been replaced; so we subtract another 5 points. Otherwise, the bear has no flaws and is in very good condition. The good-condition value we have assigned for this bear is $450. The results of the examination are as follows:

Bear A: ....100 points
Less than 10% mohair loss ....- 5
Nose floss replaced..- 5
Value rating:..90
Category: Good Condition
Correct value: $450

Picture B is a 14-inch German teddy, circa 1915. Its good-condition value is $300. When we examine the bear, we find the following:

Bear B: ....100 points
Ears backed with new acrylic fabric (an indication
that one ear was missing and the old ear was split
to make two old fronts) ....- 10
Foot & paw pads replaced with incorrect material ..- 10
40% mohair loss ....- 10
Value rating: .... 70 points
Category: Fair Condition
Correct value:..$210

The flaws on Bear B bring it down 30 points to a Fair Condition category, with a correct value of $210. One could reasonably expect to pay from $150-250 for this bear.

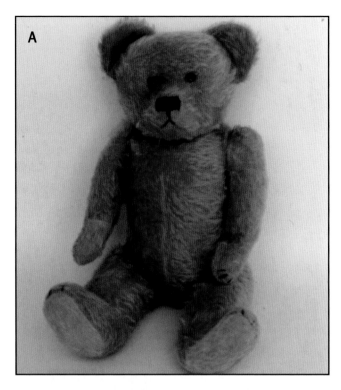

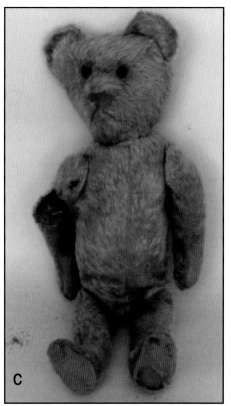
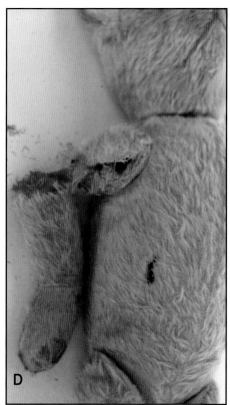

C

D

Pictures C and D show two views of our third example. It is a 24-inch British teddy, circa 1920s. Under a rating of Good Condition this bear would have a value of $300. It rates as follows:

Bear C: ....100 points
Extensive repairs to both upper arms with
incorrect thread (play damage "corrected"
by poor repair) .... - 10
Extensive mohair loss (more than 35%) .... - 10
Dry rot .... - 50

(When the bear was picked up, the arm split away, indicating extremely fragile fabric. A hole in the side of the body has also split open from slight pressure.)

Value rating: .... 30 points
Category: Poor Condition
Correct value $90

In its current state, in fact, this bear has little or no value. Dry rot does not always show itself as dramatically as in our illustration. More often than not the bear will have a rather stiff feel and small splits or cracks may be visible. Because of this problem, it is a good idea to remove any clothing from the bear and examine the body and limbs carefully. While dry rot is not a common problem, it will reduce a teddy bear to little or no value. See our chapter on Care and Feeding of Teddy Bears (page 15) for a detailed discussion of dry rot.

OTHER FACTORS AFFECTING VALUE

Just as condition factors take away from the value of a teddy bear, there are other factors that can add to its value. Most of these are not commonly found, so we have not included them in our rating scale. They include one or more of the following.

Provenance. This is any evidence of the bear's ownership history. For example, a photo of the original owner as a child with the bear adds considerably to the value. If the teddy was originally owned by some-one famous, this certainly adds great value.

Professional restoration. As noted earlier, professional restoration, or work that would be judged of professional value, does not hurt the value of a bear but enhances it. Poor workmanship, however, can hurt the value. When seeking restoration work be sure to always ask for references.

Brand name. The number-one name sought by collectors is Steiff, and this demand is reflected in the higher prices paid for this maker. Other manufacturers, such as Bing, Cramer, and numerous other producers no longer in business, are in strong demand as well.

Country of origin. It can safely be stated that bears originating in Germany are in the greatest demand. British and American bears are gaining in popularity in more recent years, as well.

Quality. If a teddy has been constructed of materials of poor quality (such as some of the carnival bears made between 1930 and the 1950s), it will not have as strong a value as a teddy crafted from mohair of good quality or other natural fibers.

Facial appeal. If you ask 100 bear collectors what the deciding factor is in their purchase, 85% are likely to say it's the facial appeal of the bear. I have seen bears in poor condition, but with that "magic look," sell for a higher price than a comparable bear in better condition with an "average" face.

The bottom line: We do not mean to imply that well-worn teddies are not worth collecting. In fact, these sometimes have the strongest character. Never buy a bear based on a predicted future value. Buy what appeals to you and it will always hold its value for you.

ANTIQUE & COLLECTIBLE
TEDDY BEAR
PRICE LISTINGS

How to Use the Price Listings

The bears are organized chronologically, by decades, and by country of origin within each period. In some group photos, there may be bears that do not belong to the country or period. If you cannot find the bear you are looking for in the proper section, it is worth checking all the group photos. In such cases, the group photo appears in the section for the earliest bear shown in the photo.

While we have given specific prices for each listing, in three conditions, the reader should assume this to be a price range and not an exact figure. Prices vary by region, by popularity of certain makers, and by the appeal of the teddy. Our goal is to establish a base price range for each bear illustrated. We have given 100% value for Good Condition, 70% for Fair Condition, and 30% for Poor Condition. The price will vary depending on the nature of the specific fault and the number of faults an individual bear has.

How to Find Your Bear

The Index, beginning on page 188, lists every bear in this book, alphabetically by maker. If you know your bear's maker, the quickest way to find it is to look up the name of the maker in the index.

If you do not know the decade, origin or maker of your bear, the following hints may help you determine the approximate age.

Material
- The earliest bears were almost always mohair.
- Cotton, wool, and wool blends indicate a bear made after 1920.
- Man-made plush and nylon blends indicate a bear made after 1945.
- Mohair in top condition probably indicates a bear made after 1980.

Eyes
- The earliest bears had shoe-button eyes.
- Blown-glass eyes were often used from the 1920s until 1945.
- Plastic eyes generally indicate a bear made after 1945.

Be sure to check the identification tips regarding specific manufacturers, which are highlighted throughout the listings.

1903-1910

Steiff, circa 1903

9 inches. Tan mohair mostly gone. Blank button. Lace shawl not original. Poor condition.

Value: Good $ 2,500
       Fair $ 1,750
       Poor $ 750

Michaud collection
Photo: T. Michaud

Steiff, circa 1904

10 inches. Tan mohair, long curved arms, long feet. Shoe-button eyes, felt pads. Blank button in ear.

Value: Good $ 4,000
       Fair $ 2,800
       Poor $ 1,200

Don and Helene Marlowe collection
Photo: Don and Helene Marlowe

Steiff, circa 1904-1906

20 inches. Excellent early example. Blank button, original pads with one small repair.

Value: Good $ 11,000
       Fair $ 7,750
       Poor $ 3,500

Sue Pearson collection
Photo: Sue Pearson

Steiff, circa 1905

16 inches. Beige mohair. Worn
foot pads.

Value: Good $ 2,000
       Fair $ 1,400
       Poor $ 600

Rare Bears collection
Photo: Karen Strickland

Steiff, circa 1905

18 inches. Beige mohair. Blank
button. Desirable size.

Value: Good $ 2,200
       Fair $ 1,550
       Poor $ 650

Rare Bears collection
Photo: Karen Strickland

Steiff, circa 1905

24 inches

Value: Good $ 10,500
       Fair $ 7,350
       Poor $ 3,150

Linda Mullins collection
Photo: Linda Mullins

Steiff, circa 1905-07

Small bear: 8½ inches. Cream mohair, long curved arms, long feet. Replaced felt pads. Re-stitched nose and mouth. Shoe-button eyes.

Value: Good $ 1,600
       Fair $ 1,125
       Poor $ 475

Larger bear: 11 inches. White mohair, brown floss nose and claws, long curved arms, long feet. Shoe-button eyes.

Value: Good $ 1,500
       Fair $ 1,050
       Poor $ 500

Don and Helene Marlowe collection
Photo: Don and Helene Marlowe

Note: Large bear is wearing an authentic Teddy G Rough Rider outfit, circa 1907 (not original to bear). Outfit is rare.

Value of outfit alone:
    Good $ 400
    Fair $ 275
    Poor $ 125

❖Steiff blank buttons are usually an indication of one of their early bears (1903-1906) but there are exceptions. One of the Steiff officials indicated that it was not unheard of for them to use the blank button when a supply of printed buttons ran out.

    Readers should also be aware that Steiff currently uses a blank brass button in pieces that are sold in their factory store in Germany and are deemed of secondary quality. We have carefully examined several pieces from this store and were not able to detect any flaws.

Steiff, circa 1906

16 inches. White mohair. (Many
early Steiff bears described as
being white mohair are actually
a pale beige color). Cardboard
inserts in feet. Superb condition.

Value: Good $ 6,500
      Fair $ 4,550
      Poor $ 1,950

Sally Carolous collection
Photo: Judi Dolan

Steiff, circa 1907

8 inches. This well-loved teddy was
the constant companion of a young
boy who enjoyed his company until
his later years.

Value: Good $ 2,000
      Fair $ 1,400
      Poor $ 600

Delores Buntz collection
Photo: Robert Buntz

Steiff, circa 1907

14 inches. Tan mohair.

Value: Good $ 1,400
      Fair $ 1,000
      Poor $ 425

Delores Buntz collection
Photo: Robert Buntz

Steiff, circa 1907

16 inches. Condition is very good.
Button in ear.

Value: Good $ 4,500
        Fair $ 3,150
        Poor $ 1,350

Sue Pearson collection
Photo: Sue Pearson

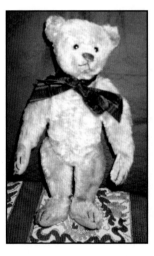

Steiff, circa 1907

12 inches. Original pads. Slight
mohair loss. No button.

Value: Good $ 2,800
        Fair $ 1,950
        Poor $ 850

Judi Dolan collection
Photo: Judi Dolan

Steiff, circa 1907

14 inches. White mohair.
Blank button.

Value: Good $ 2,500
        Fair $ 1,750
        Poor $ 750

Rare Bears collection
Photo: Karen Strickland

Steiff, circa 1907

20 inches. Light-caramel mohair.
Felt pads. Typical long curved
arms.

Value: Good $ 2,800
      Fair $ 1,950
      Poor $ 850

Rare Bears collection
Photo: Karen Strickland

Steiff, circa 1908

20 inches. All original with button.
A very desirable bear.

Value: Good $ 10,000
      Fair $ 7,000
      Poor $ 3,000

Sue Pearson collection
Photo: Sue Pearson

Steiff, circa 1908

9½ inches. White mohair (actually
pale beige). Highly desirable size.
Ff button.

Value: Good $ 2,200
      Fair $ 1,550
      Poor $ 650

Michaud collection
Photo: T. Michaud

Steiff, circa 1909

14 inches. Bright gold. Slight mohair loss. Provenance: reported to have been found in a "house of ill repute" in Germany!

Value: Good $ 4,000
Fair $ 2,800
Poor $ 1,200

Judi Dolan collection
Photo: Judi Dolan

Steiff center seam, circa 1909

20 inches. Cinnamon-brown long mohair. Wool felt pads, black shoe-button eyes. Straw stuffing.

Value: Good $ 4,800
Fair $ 3,360
Poor $ 1,450

Dolls and Bears of Charlton Court collection
Photo: Adrienne Zisser

Steiff, circa 1910

10 inches. Light-tan mohair, shoe-button eyes, long curved arms. Felt pads. Sweater not original.

Value: Good $ 1,500
Fair $ 1,000
Poor $ 450

Don and Helene Marlowe collection
Photo: Don and Helene Marlowe

❖ Some of Steiff's early bears featured a center seam right down the center of the head to the nose. This was done to utilize smaller pieces of mohair that would otherwise have been discarded. Only a small percent of their early production featured this design, and these bring premium prices.

Steiff, circa 1910

14 inches. Beige mohair.
Pronounced floss claws on feet
and paws.

Value: Good $ 1,800
        Fair $ 1,250
        Poor $ 550

Rare Bears collection
Photo: Karen Strickland

Steiff, circa 1910

6 inches. Referred to as the "cone
nose" bear. Short light-brown
mohair. No foot or paw pads.

Value: Good $ 750
        Fair $ 525
        Poor $ 225

Rare Bears collection
Photo: Karen Strickland

Steiff, circa 1910

10 inches. Repairs to nose and
neck. Mohair is completely gone.
Button in the ear. (This bear was
so bald that Doris knitted an
outfit for it.)

Value: Good $ 1,200
        Fair $ 850
        Poor $ 350

Michaud collection
Photo: T. Michaud

41

Steiff, circa 1910

12 inches. Sparse cinnamon mohair. Clear glass eyes with black centers (probably were painted backs). Long curved arms. Legs tapered to an ankle, long feet. Felt pads. 5 claws on feet and paws. Button in ear missing. Bear shown is in fair condition.

Value: Good $ 1,600
Fair $ 1,100
Poor $ 500

Helen (Peggy) Williams collection
Photo: Peggy Williams

Maker unknown, circa 1905

13 inches. Tan mohair. Shoe-button eyes. Some wear, but still a charmer.

Value: Good $ 1,000
Fair $ 700
Poor $ 300

Michaud collection
Photo : T. Michaud

Maker unknown, bear on wheels, circa 1910

9 inches long

Value: Good $ 900
Fair $ 650
Poor $ 275

Delores Buntz collection
Photo: Robert Buntz

Steiff, bi-color bear, circa 1926

24 inches

Value:	Good	$ 25,000
	Fair	$ 17,500
	Poor	$ 7,500

Steiff, circa 1907

24 inches

Value:	Good	$ 15,000
	Fair	$ 10,000
	Poor	$ 4,500

Linda Mullins collection
Photo: Linda Mullins

Additional Listing, not pictured

Steiff, bear on wheels, circa 1908

9 inches high at shoulder. Off-white mohair. No button. Some wear.

Value:	Good	$ 1,600
	Fair	$ 1,100
	Poor	$ 600

❖Some of Steiff's earliest bears (1903-04) were jointed by a rod mechanism. They are referred to as rod bears and bring premium prices. If you suspect you have such a bear, an x-ray will disclose the metal rods if they are present.

Ideal, circa 1906

This bear is a perfect example of how provenance can greatly enhance the value of a teddy bear. This is the actual model that was chosen by the U.S. Post Office to serve as the image on their "Celebrate the Century" stamp series issued early 1998.

Value: Good	$	1,300
With provenance	$	2,000
Fair	$	900
Poor	$	400

Dee Hockenberry collection
Photo: Tom Hockenberry

Limited edition of 1906 American bear used in the U.S. Postal "Celebrate the Century" series. This teddy was co-designed by Frances Harper and Dee Hockenberry to give collectors the opportunity to own a piece of history. Edition of 2000.
10 inches tall in mohair. Fully jointed. Excelsior stuffed. Embroidered felt pads. Presentation box. Signed.

Value: $149 issue price

Dee Hockenberry collection
Photo: Tom Hockenberry

❖Many of the early Ideal bears are recognizable by their unusual oval foot pads, which come to a point at the top. They are also likely to have a rather pronounced triangular head gusset. Ears are typically large and set wide apart.

Left: Ideal, circa 1909

14 inches. Gold mohair, glass eyes, felt pads. Twill nose and mouth.

Value: Good $ 1,000
       Fair $ 700
       Poor $ 300

Right: Teddy Girl, circa 1910

9 inches. Red mohair, celluloid face. Blond hair under hood. These bears are considered quite rare as they were only produced for a few years.

Value: Good $ 400
       Fair $ 275
       Poor $ 125

Dolls and Bears of Charlton Court collection
Photo: Adrienne Zisser

Ideal, circa 1910

24 inches. This wonderful teddy comes with a photo of the original owner, which adds significantly to the value.

Value: Good $ 1,000
     With provenance $ 1,500
           Fair $ 750
          Poor $ 350

Jo Nell Harkrider collection
Photo: Robert Buntz

Maker unknown, circa 1905

15 inches. Old gold mohair, fat football body. Triangular-shaped head with low-set ears. Shoe-button eyes. Curved arms. Large feet with cardboard insole. Portion of red tongue remains.

Value: Good $ 1,500
       Fair $ 1,000
       Poor $ 450

Don and Helene Marlowe collection
Photo: Don and Helene Marlowe

Hecla, circa 1907

16 inches. White mohair with rust floss on nose and paws.

Value: Good $ 2,800
       Fair $ 1,950
       Poor $ 850

Mort and Evelyn Wood collection
Photo: Mort Wood

Maker unknown (possibly Bruin), circa 1907

12 inches

Value: Good $ 1,800
        Fair $ 1,250
        Poor $ 550

Mort and Evelyn Wood collection
Photo: Mort Wood

Maker unknown (possibly Ideal), circa 1905

13 inches. Short gold mohair, triangular-shaped head. Low-set ears. Brown shoe-button eyes. Long curved arms, felt pads on feet come to a point at top.

Value: Good $ 800
        Fair $ 550
        Poor $ 250

Don and Helene Marlowe collection
Photo: Don and Helene Marlowe

❖A stamped ID "Aetna" was placed on the right food pad by this American firm, dating from 1907. Frequently the name will be worn, but traces can sometimes still be found.

Maker unknown, circa 1910

Large bear, 25 inches. Short gold mohair, felt pads, large ears, glass eyes.

Value:
Good	$	400
Fair	$	275
Poor	$	125

Small bear, 11 inches. White mohair, felt pads, amber glass eyes. Replaced ears.

Value:
Good	$	250
Fair	$	175
Poor	$	75

Don and Helene Marlowe collection
Photo: Don and Helene Marlowe

Maker unknown, circa 1910

18 inches. Superior materials and quality.

Value:
Good	$	3,000
Fair	$	2,100
Poor	$	900

Mort and Evelyn Wood collection
Photo: Mort Wood

Maker unknown, circa 1910

13 inches. Very well-loved bear (most of mohair is gone). Pronounced hump, extremely elongated snout (missing mohair emphasizes length of nose). Tiny black glass eyes. Large low-set ears, replaced foot pads.

Value:
Good	$	350
Fair	$	250
Poor	$	100

Don and Helene Marlowe collection
Photo: Don and Helene Marlowe

Maker unknown (possibly Miller Mfg.), circa 1908

14 inches. Characteristic wool plush for this company.

Value:
Good	$	1,800
Fair	$	1,250
Poor	$	550

Mort and Evelyn Wood collection
Photo: Mort Wood

Maker unknown, circa 1910

14 inches. Caramel mohair, shoe-button eyes, felt pads. Long feet. Low-set ears on triangular-shaped head. This shape was used by Ideal and by Bruin Manufacturing Co.

Value:
Good	$	975
Fair	$	700
Poor	$	300

Don and Helene Marlowe collection
Photo: Don and Helene Marlowe

JK Farnell, circa 1910

13 inches. Great example of an early Farnell.

Value:		
Good	$	2,500
Fair	$	1,750
Poor	$	750

JK Farnell, circa 1907

13 inches. Earlier Farnell in mint condition.

Value:		
Good	$	3,100
Fair	$	2,175
Poor	$	950

Sue Pearson collection
Photo: Sue Pearson

Maker unknown (France), musical polar bear, circa 1890-1910

6 inches long. Papier-mâché-and-wood bear on all fours, covered in white mohair. Molded open mouth with painted teeth, amber glass eyes. Tail is a metal crank covered with leather that is turned to play music. Working condition. May be Roullet-Decamps.

Value: Good $ 1,800
       Fair $ 1,250
       Poor $ 550

Don and Helene Marlowe collection
Photo: Don and Helene Marlowe

Maker unknown, electric-eye bear, circa 1910

18 inches. Light-bulb eyes operated by a battery sewn into body (battery missing). Cotton twill nose. Felt pads. Note: while the eyes do not work, this is an exceptional example of an electric-eye bear.

Value: Good $ 1,200
       Fair $ 850
       Poor $ 350

Helen (Peggy) Williams collection
Photo: Peggy Williams

Additional Listings, not pictured

Maker unkown, electric-eye bear, circa 1907-1910

22 inches. Medium-dark-brown mohair. Jointed arms, unjointed legs and head. Straw stuffing. Press a switch in his tummy and the eyes light. Battery sewn inside back.

Value: Good $ 1,500
       Fair $ 1,000
       Poor $ 400

Roullet & Decamps (France), mechanical bear, circa 1905

12 inches. Papier-mâché molded body contains drive mechanism that allows bear to perform tumbling feats on a trapeze. Rare.

Value: Good $ 6,000
       Fair $ 4,500
       Poor $ 1,500

Maker unknown (England), circa 1908

8 inches. Light-gold mohair. Ears are tucked into a small hole in head. While this feature is attributed to several German makers, it was copied by producers in other countries. Jointed. Short arms, long legs. Flat facial features.

Value: Good $ 1,000
       Fair $ 700
       Poor $ 250

Maker unknown (France), circa 1908

6 inches. Cinnamon mohair. Wire-pin jointed arms and legs. Unjointed head. Tiny solid black eyes.

Value: Good $ 600
       Fair $ 400
       Poor $ 150

Maker unknown, bear on wheels, circa 1910

16 inches long. Unusual fabric is a flat nap wool, similar to fabric used for upholstery in that era. Shoe-button eyes. Jointed head. Mounted on axles with cast iron wheels.

Value: Good $ 800
       Fair $ 550
       Poor $ 200

1910-1920

Bing, circa 1920

20 inches. Desirable size. No button,
but all Bing characteristics.

Value: Good $ 4,500
       Fair $ 3,150
       Poor $ 1,350

Mort and Evelyn Wood collection
Photo: Mort Wood

Bing, circa 1915

14 inches. No ID marks, but all
Bing characteristics.

Value: Good $ 1,500
       Fair $ 1,000
       Poor $ 400

Mort and Evelyn Wood collection
Photo: Mort Wood

❖ Bing bears have a small trademark button placed under the left arm or in the right ear with the initials GBN on it. This was done from around 1907 to the early 1920s; after that date the button was placed on the arm or body. Bing used shoe-button eyes until the 1920s, and glass eyes after that era. Many Bing bears are considered quite rare, and can bring prices equal to, or greater than, Steiff bears.

Schuco, yes/no bear, circa 1920

7 inches. Head makes yes or no motion by movement of the tail.

Value: Good $ 800
       Fair $ 550
       Poor $ 250

Delores Buntz collection
Photo: Robert Buntz

Schuco, yes/no bear, circa 1920

20 inches. Gold mohair, glass eyes. Replaced linen pads. Excelsior stuffing.

Value: Good $ 1,200
       Fair $ 850
       Poor $ 350

Dee Hockenberry collection
Photo: Tom Hockenberry

JOPI, circa 1920

24 inches. Large glass eyes, soft expression, superior workmanship. Initials JOPI represent company name: Josef Pitrmann.

Value:		
Good	$	6,500
Fair	$	4,550
Poor	$	1,950

Mort and Evelyn Wood collection
Photo: Mort Wood

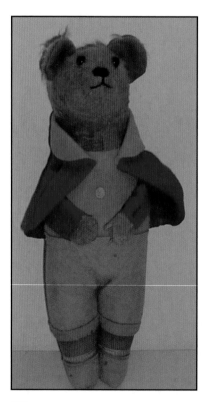

Petz, circa 1920

11 inches. This unique teddy has a mohair head and the original felt outfit, which is part of the bear. Glass eyes. Unjointed.

Value:		
Good	$	150
Fair	$	100
Poor	$	50

Susan and Steve Swickard collection
Photo: T. Michaud

Steiff, circa 1920

20 inches. Pale-beige mohair.
Ff button.

Value: Good $ 2,500
      Fair $ 1,750
      Poor $ 750

Rare Bears collection
Photo: Karen Strickland

Maker unknown, bear on wheels, circa 1915

6½ inches long. Mohair over papier-mâché body. Tin wheels. Photo shows original owners, twin boys, with one of them holding the bear on wheels.

Value: Good $ 350
With provenance $ 525
      Fair $ 250
      Poor $ 100

Michaud collection
Photo: T. Michaud

Steiff, circa 1915

8 inches. Tan mohair.
A popular size.

Value: Good $ 2,000
        Fair $ 1,500
        Poor $ 600

Jo Nell Harkrider collection
Photo: Robert Buntz

Steiff, muff, circa 1915

Rare.

Value: Good $ 1,000
        Fair $ 700
        Poor $ 300

Kaye Mason collection
Photo: Robert Buntz

❖ Examine the bear's left ear closely to see if it has a hole indicating that a Steiff button may have been removed. Please note that if a hole has been punched in the ear with a nail or similar object, the hole is usually very clean. If a Steiff button was removed many years ago, the hole will have traces of dirt or stain around it.

Maker unknown, circa 1915

26 inches. Has some facial characteristics of Bing. Other marked differences. The face says "Take me home!"

Value: Good $ 3,000
       Fair $ 2,100
       Poor $ 900

Mort and Evelyn Wood collection
Photo: Mort Wood

Maker unknown, circa 1915

20 inches. Faded-pink curly mohair. Excelsior stuffing. Large cup-shaped ears sewn across head seam. Black shoe-button eyes. Nose and mouth of rust pearl cotton. Football-shaped body. Hard board discs in feet. Rust claws.

Value: Good $ 1,500
       Fair $ 1,000
       Poor $ 400

Helen (Peggy) Williams collection
Photo: Peggy Williams

Ideal, circa 1915

22 inches. Short sparse red mohair. Excelsior stuffing. Slender upturned arms, long slender legs.

Value: Good $ 800
       Fair $ 550
       Poor $ 250

Helen (Peggy) Williams collection
Photo: Peggy Williams

Maker unknown, circa 1915

14 inches. Tan mohair. Replaced pads. Some balding. Fair condition.

Value: Good $ 250
       Fair $ 175
       Poor $ 75

Michaud collection
Photo: T. Michaud

Maker unknown, circa 1915

17 inches. Short gold bristly mohair. Football-shaped body. Ears gathered and tucked into head opening

Value: Good $ 600
       Fair $ 425
       Poor $ 175

Helen (Peggy) Williams collection
Photo: Peggy Williams

Maker unknown, circa 1918

25 inches. Gold mohair. Felt pads replaced. Football-shaped body. Small feet. Typical characteristics of American bears of this era.

Value:			
	Good	$	450
	Fair	$	300
	Poor	$	125

Dee Hockenberry collection
Photo: Tom Hockenberry

Maker unknown, circa 1920

19 inches. Short nap, pale-gold mohair.

Value:			
	Good	$	350
	Fair	$	250
	Poor	$	100

Michaud collection
Photo: T. Michaud

Chad Valley, circa 1920s

14 inches. Light-gold long mohair.
Flannel pads. Head has straw stuffing;
body has straw and cotton stuffing.
Button on chest reads: Aerolite - Chad
Valley. Bear shown is in fair condition.

Value:	Good	$	350
	Fair	$	250
	Poor	$	100

Dolls and Bears of Charlton Court collection
Photo: Adrienne Zisser

❖Bears with straw-stuffed heads and soft stuffed (cotton or kapok) bodies are usually of British origin.

Additional Listings, not pictured

JK Farnell, circa 1918

14 inches. Light tan mohair.
Jointed.

Value: Good $ 2,500
      Fair $ 1,800
      Poor $ 800

JK Farnell, circa 1918

28 inches. Light-gold mohair.
Shaved muzzle. Webbed stitching
on pads for claws, typical of the early
Farnell bears. Large glass eyes.

Value: Good $ 3,500
      Fair $ 2,500
      Poor $ 1,000

JK Farnell, circa 1920

16 inches. Long beige mohair.
Shaved muzzle. Large ears. Webbed
claw stitching. Light rust-colored
nose stitched horizontally.
Cardboard inserts in feet.

Value: Good $ 2,500
      Fair $ 1,800
      Poor $ 750

Maker unknown (England), circa 1914

11 inches. Mohair. Jointed.

Value: Good $ 600
      Fair $ 400
      Poor $ 200

❖ From the early days on through the 1930s, British teddy bears tended to have shorter arms than their German counterparts. Eyes were usually glass, with occasional metal, rather than shoe-button, eyes used. British manufacturers got a big boost in sales during World War I when imported German bears (and other products) were banned.

Maker unknown (Canada, possibly Dominion), circa 1920

20 inches. Short sparse gold mohair. Excelsior stuffing. Tiny ears tucked into head seams. Long thin torso, short thin arms with upturned paws. Straight legs with short feet.

Value: Good $ 400
Fair $ 275
Poor $ 125

Helen (Peggy) Williams collection
Photo: Peggy Williams

Dominion, (Canada) circa 1920

30 inches. Sparse pink mohair. Excelsior stuffing. Tapered arms with upturned paws. Straight legs with short feet.

Value: Good $ 600
Fair $ 425
Poor $ 175

Helen (Peggy) Williams collection
Photo: Peggy Williams

FADAP, (France) circa 1920

23 inches. Curly mohair, glass eyes. Bat-shaped nose. Initials stand for: "Fabrication Artistique d' Animaux en Peluche."

Value: Good $ 1,400
Fair $ 1,000
Poor $ 400

Mort and Evelyn Wood collection
Photo: Mort Wood

1920-1930

Eduard Cramer, circa 1929

14 inches. Reddish-gold mohair. Brown nose stitching, red mouth stitching. This is the rare Cramer mechanical walking bear.

Value:
Good $ 4,500
Fair $ 3,150
Poor $ 1,350

Rare Bears collection
Photo: Karen Strickland

Eduard Cramer, circa 1930

17 inches. Tilt-head musical movement. A highly desirable bear.

Value:
Good $ 2,200
Fair $ 1,550
Poor $ 650

Mort and Evelyn Wood collection
Photo: Mort Wood

Petz, circa 1926

18 inches. Cinnamon mohair.

Value:
Good $ 500
Fair $ 350
Poor $ 150

Delores Buntz collection
Photo: Robert Buntz

Schuco, miniature, circa 1920s

2¼ inches. One of Schuco's earlier miniatures, as attested by the felt paws and feet protruding from the bear. Rare.

Value: Good $ 400
       Fair $ 275
       Poor $ 125

Michaud collection
Photo: T. Michaud

Schuco, bell hop, circa 1923

18 inches. One of the most sought-after of Shuco's mechanical bears.

Value: Good $ 4,000
       Fair $ 2,750
       Poor $ 1,200

Jo Nell Harkrider collection
Photo: Robert Buntz

Schuco, miniature yes/no bear, circa 1930

4¾ inches. Mechanism operated by tail. Mohair over metal framework. Velvet feet with painted details. Tail cover missing.

Value: Good $ 600
       Fair $ 425
       Poor $ 175

Helen (Peggy) Williams collection
Photo: Peggy Williams

Schuco, perfume and compact bears, circa 1920s

Perfume, 5 inches; compact, 3½ inches. Displayed in tin lithographed toy buggy.

Value (perfume):	Good	$	700
	Fair	$	500
	Poor	$	200
Value (compact):	Good	$	900
	Fair	$	650
	Poor	$	275

Delores Buntz collection
Photo: Robert Buntz

Schuco, perfume and compact bears, circa 1920s

Perfume (in wagon): 4½ inches, removes head to reveal a perfume vial in body. Compact (front): 3½ inches, opens to reveal a lipstick in the neck and a compact in the body.

Value (each):	Good	$	900
	Fair	$	650
	Poor	$	275

Jo Nell Harkrider collection
Photo: Robert Buntz

Schuco, yes/no bear and fox, circa 1920s

Bear: 11 inches, fat football-shaped body, small ears set on top of head, shoe-button eyes, short-nap gold mohair.

Value:	Good	$	1,500
	Fair	$	1,000
	Poor	$	450

Yes/no fox: 6 inches, short brown-and-white mohair, green glass eyes.

Value:	Good	$	800
	Fair	$	550
	Poor	$	250

Don and Helene Marlowe collection
Photo: Don and Helene Marlowe

Steiff, bear on wheels, circa 1920s

14 inches long, 10 inches high.

Value: Good $ 1,600
Fair $ 1,125
Poor $ 500

Jo Nell Harkrider collection
Photo: Robert Buntz

Steiff, gallop bear on wheels, circa 1920s

4 inches. Short tan mohair bear on eccentric wood wheels. Tiny amber glass eyes, button in ear.

Value: Good $ 2,800
Fair $ 1,950
Poor $ 850

Don and Helene Marlowe collection
Photo: Don and Helene Marlowe

Steiff Petsy, circa 1928

9½ inches. Long brown-tipped mohair. Long arms, large feet. Rose-colored floss nose (worn), matching claw color. Replaced pads. Hard to find in this size. New miniature Steiff shown for size comparison.

Value: Good $ 1,600
Fair $ 1,100
Poor $ 500

Don and Helene Marlowe collection
Photo: Don & Helene Marlowe

Steiff, circa 1920s

10 inches. Tan mohair.

Value: Good $ 1,200
       Fair $ 850
       Poor $ 350

Delores Buntz collection
Photo: Robert Buntz

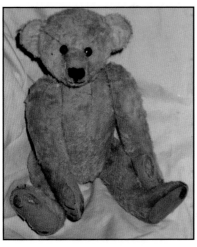

Steiff, circa 1920s

19 inches. Tan mohair,
shoe-button eyes.

Value: Good $ 2,400
       Fair $ 1,675
       Poor $ 725

Beverly Vye collection
Photo: Donna McPherson

Steiff, circa 1920s

13 inches. Light-gold mohair.
No button. Scarf not original.

Value: Good $ 1,000
       Fair $ 700
       Poor $ 300

Michaud collection
Photo: T. Michaud

Left: Maker unknown, circa 1920s

20 inches. Gold mohair. Outfit not original. Some damage to wrists.

Value:	Good	$	500
	Fair	$	350
	Poor	$	150

Center: Maker unknown (England), circa 1930s

23 inches. Long golden mohair. Original pads. Outfit not original.

Value:	Good	$	600
	Fair	$	400
	Poor	$	150

Right: Maker unknown (United States), circa 1936

20 inches. Age is specific, as he comes from original owner. Eyes were replaced many years ago with common buttons. Replaced pads. Well-loved condition. The value lost to condition is more than made up by the bear's provenance.

Value:	Good	$	450
With provenance		$	600
	Fair	$	325
	Poor	$	125

Michaud Collection
Photo: T. Michaud

Steiff, rattle bear, circa 1920s

5 inches. Short-nap white mohair, long upturned feet with no pads. Straight arms. Brown stitched nose and mouth, amber glass eyes. Braided leather collar appears to be original. Bear is actually a baby rattle with loose pellets (probably metal) inside the tummy.

Value:	Good	$	1,800
	Fair	$	1,250
	Poor	$	550

Don & Helene Marlowe collection
Photo: Don & Helene Marlowe

Maker unknown, circa 1920s

14 inches. Tan mohair. Shoe-button eyes. Outfit not original.

Value:	Good	$	400
	Fair	$	275
	Poor	$	125

Michaud collection
Photo: T. Michaud

Maker unknown, circa 1920s

22 inches. This bear has all the characteristics of a JOPI bear and has a musical squeeze bellows movement. Tipped mohair.

Value:	Good	$	3,300
	Fair	$	2,300
	Poor	$	1,000

Sue Pearson collection
Photo: Sue Pearson

Maker unknown, circa 1920s

10 inches. Medium-length pale-beige mohair. Shawl not original. Purchased from original owner with picture of her as a child. Bear is named Aunt Eunice after original owner.

Value: Good	$	300
With provenance	$	375
Fair	$	200
Poor	$	100

Michaud collection
Photo: T. Michaud

Maker unknown, bear on wheels, circa 1920s

16 inches long, 12 inches high. Iron wheels. Bear has short-nap beige mohair, glass eyes. Leather collar. Carriage and collar not original.

Value: Good	$	850
Fair	$	600
Poor	$	250

Michaud collection
Photo: T. Michaud

Maker unknown, circa 1930

29 inches. Possibly inspired by Steiff Dickie bear.

Value: Good	$	2,800
Fair	$	2,000
Poor	$	850

Mort and Evelyn Wood collection
Photo: Mort Wood

Helvetic, circa 1920s

12 inches. Long golden mohair, large amber glass eyes, kapok stuffing. Wool felt pads (in bad condition). This company made a number of musical bears with squeeze bellows mechanism, but this is not one of them.

Value: Good $ 400
       Fair $ 275
       Poor $ 125

Donna McPherson collection
Photo: Donna McPherson

Ideal, circa 1920s

10 inches. Short dark-gold mohair, shoe-button eyes. Large ears, twill nose. Short straight arms. Metal disc joints.

Value: Good $ 450
       Fair $ 325
       Poor $ 125

Don and Helene Marlowe collection
Photo: Don and Helene Marlowe

❖ If you have a teddy that plays music (Swiss music-box type) when you squeeze his tummy, it could well be a Helvetic teddy bear. This American firm imported the music boxes from Switzerland. The bears typically had a large body and broad chest to accommodate the music-box mechanism. Helvetic company produced teddy bears in the mid 1920s.

Left: Maker unknown, circa 1920s

16 inches. Short-nap gold mohair. Typical short arms, little shape to feet. Boots and scarf not original.

Value: Good $ 450
Fair $ 325
Poor $ 125

Center: Pedigree (Ireland), circa 1950s

16 inches. Gold mohair, brown velvet pads. Original label on back of neck. Pedigree started production in England, then moved to Ireland and had produc-tion facilities in other countries as well. Felt hat not original.

Value: Good $ 500
Fair $ 350
Poor $ 150

Right: Knickerbocker, circa 1940s

16 inches. Typical rust mohair. Obtained from original owner.

Value: Good $ 300
Fair $ 200
Poor $ 100

Michaud collection
Photo: T. Michaud

Maker unknown, circa 1920s

17 inches. Gold short mohair, shoe-button eyes. No shape to feet (typical of some conservative cottage industry companies). Bear shown is in fair condition.

Value: Good $ 550
Fair $ 400
Poor $ 175

Dolls and Bears of Charlton Court collection
Photo: Adrienne Zisser

Knickerbocker, circa 1930

23 inches. Cinnamon mohair.

Value: Good $ 400
      Fair $ 275
      Poor $ 125

Jo Nell Harkrider collection
Photo: Robert Buntz

❖ Knickerbocker started business in 1850, producing lithographed alphabet blocks. After the turn of the century, when teddy became popular, they joined other U.S. firms in crafting teddy bears. Many of the Knickerbocker bears have a sewn-in muzzle of short-nap mohair in contrast to the longer mohair used in the rest of the bear. Paw pads are frequently made of velveteen. Arms are short and feet are not pronounced. Cinnamon was a popular mohair color for this firm.

Maker unknown, clown, circa 1920s

11 inches. Pink-and-white short mohair, stubby feet, straight arms. Small amber glass eyes, small sliced-in ears, felt pads. Original pleated cotton neck ruff. Missing hat.

Value: Good $ 800
      Fair $ 550
      Poor $ 250

Don and Helene Marlowe collection
Photo: Don and Helene Marlowe

Maker unknown (possibly Knickerbocker), circa 1920s

20 inches. Long reddish-gold mohair. Very good condition. Bear was found in the back room of an old country store.

Value: Good $ 500
        Fair $ 350
        Poor $ 150

Michaud collection
Photo: T. Michaud

Maker unknown, stick bear, circa 1920s

9½ inches. Short, sparse mohair. Short arms, short legs with little shape to foot.

Value: Good $ 200
        Fair $ 150
        Poor $ 50

Michaud collection
Photo: T. Michaud

Maker unknown, circa 1920s

17 inches. Short sparse faded-pink mohair. Shoe-button eyes, felt pads, stubby feet. Sliced-in ears (tucked into small opening in head).

Value: Good $ 350
        Fair $ 250
        Poor $ 100

Don and Helene Marlowe collection
Photo: Don and Helene Marlowe

Left: **Maker and origin unknown, circa 1920s**
12 inches. Shoe-button eyes. Wool fabric. Replaced pads. Excessive wear. Sweater not original.

Value: Good $ 150
        Fair $ 100
        Poor $ 50

Center: **Commonwealth Toy Co. Feed Me Bear, circa 1930s**
14 inches. Mohair. When mouth is opened by pulling on a brass ring at the back of the head, teddy opens wide and food can be fed into a metal tube.

Turn him over and open a zipper at the back to retrieve the food. Rare. Bib is a recreation of the original.

Value: Good $ 1,000
        Fair $ 750
        Poor $ 300

Right: **Maker unknown, circa 1920s**
15 inches. Light-tan mohair. Pads replaced. Worn condition.

Value: Good $ 500
        Fair $ 350
        Poor $ 150

Michaud collection
Photo: T. Michaud

Maker unknown, muff, circa 1920s

7 inches wide, 9 inches tall. Rare early example.

Value: Good $ 600
        Fair $ 425
        Poor $ 175

Michaud collection
Photo: T. Michaud

Maker unknown, circa 1930

22 inches. Curly bright-gold mohair. Excelsior stuffing. Elongated body with prominent chest. Straight legs with short, stubby feet. Long thin arms with curved paws. Felt pads. Shoe-button eyes.

Value: Good $ 500
      Fair $ 350
      Poor $ 150

Helen (Peggy) Williams collection.
Photo: Peggy Williams

Left: Maker unknown, circa 1940s

15 inches. White mohair. Celluloid eyes. Sweater not original.

Value: Good $ 300
      Fair $ 200
      Poor $ 100

Center: Maker unknown, circa 1920s

14 inches. Pale-gold mohair. Replaced pads. Sweater not original.

Value: Good $ 400
      Fair $ 275
      Poor $ 125

Right: Maker unknown (England), circa 1920s

10 inches. Well-worn gold mohair. Glass eyes. Wearing an old velvet hat (not original).

Value: Good $ 350
      Fair $ 250
      Poor $ 100

Michaud collection
Photo: T. Michaud

Maker unknown, circa 1920s

15 inches. Light-gold mohair, long curved arms, felt pads. Large cupped ears, clipped snout. Amber glass eyes.

Value: Good $ 400
Fair $ 275
Poor $ 125

Don and Helene Marlowe collection
Photo: Don and Helene Marlowe

Maker unknown, circa 1920s

Large bear, 13 inches. Cinnamon mohair, replaced pads. Clipped upturned snout, shoe-button eyes.

Value: Good $ 350
Fair $ 225
Poor $ 100

Small bear, 9½ inches. Short gold mohair, short arms, stubby feet. Replaced pads. Low-set ears on side of head. Shoe-button eyes.

Value: Good $ 250
Fair $ 175
Poor $ 75

Don and Helene Marlowe collection
Photo: Don and Helene Marlowe

Maker unknown, circa 1930

18 inches. Gold silky mohair. Straight and short arms and legs. Three black claws on paws and feet. Beige felt pads.

Value: Good $ 400
Fair $ 275
Poor $ 125

Helen (Peggy) Williams collection
Photo: Peggy Williams

Chad Valley, panda, circa 1930

13 inches. Black-and-white mohair. This panda has his original label on his foot and is considered a rare find. Brown floss nose.

Value: Good $ 1,200
       Fair $ 850
       Poor $ 350

Sue Pearson collection
Photo: Sue Pearson

Chad Valley, circa 1930

27 inches. ID tag on foot and celluloid button in right ear.

Value: Good $ 2,300
       Fair $ 1,600
       Poor $ 700

Mort and Evelyn Wood collection
Photo: Mort Wood

Chiltern, circa 1920s

18 inches. Chiltern teddies (and in fact most British bears) have come into greater demand by collectors in recent years. This fellow has little mohair left, so he wears a robe to keep warm.

Value: Good $ 700
       Fair $ 500
       Poor $ 200

Jo Nell Harkrider collection
Photo: Robert Buntz

Maker unknown, circa 1920s

18 inches. Clear glass eyes.

Value:	Good	$	500
	Fair	$	350
	Poor	$	150

Sue Pearson collection
Photo: Sue Pearson

Maker unknown, circa 1920s

15 inches. Light-gold mohair, amber glass eyes, felt pads. Long arms. Nightshirt and slippers not original.

Value:	Good	$	375
	Fair	$	250
	Poor	$	125

Don and Helene Marlowe collection
Photo: Don and Helene Marlowe

Maker unknown, circa 1920s

22 inches. Yellow-gold mohair (some-what faded), curved arms, cup-shaped ears, beautiful original blue glass eyes. Replaced paw pads.

Value:	Good	$	500
	Fair	$	350
	Poor	$	150

Don and Helene Marlowe collection
Photo: Don and Helene Marlowe

JK Farnell, circa 1920s

18 inches

Value: Good $ 800
      Fair $ 550
      Poor $ 250

Jo Nell Harkrider collection
Photo: Robert Buntz

JK Farnell, circa 1923

18 inches. Wears early leggings (not original).
Has original paper chest tag that says "I Growl."
The original Winnie-the-Pooh bear was
reported to be a Farnell.

Value: Good $ 2,200
      Fair $ 1,550
      Poor $ 650

Judi Dolan collection
Photo: Judi Dolan

JK Farnell, circa 1930

22 inches. Blond mohair, glass eyes.
Linen pads. Kapok stuffing.

Value: Good $ 2,000
      Fair $ 1,400
      Poor $ 600

Dee Hockenberry collection
Photo: Tom Hockenberry

❖ Early Alpha Farnell Bears are sometimes misidentified as Steiff because the company did, in fact, utilize many of the same characteristics as did Steiff. An embroidered label was attached to the left foot pad, and even if it has been removed you can frequently see the outline of where it was located.

Left: Maker unknown, circa 1920s

11 inches. Yellow knit dress not original.

Value: Good $ 350
       Fair $ 250
       Poor $ 100

Right: Maker unknown, circa 1920s

17 inches. Wears Edwardian smock.

Value: Good $ 475
       Fair $ 325
       Poor $ 125

Sue Pearson collection
Photo: Sue Pearson

Maker unknown, circa 1920s

24 inches. Medium-length gold mohair. Body and leg repairs. Bear shown is in fair to poor condition.

Value: Good $ 450
       Fair $ 325
       Poor $ 125

Michaud collection
Photo: T. Michaud

Maker unknown, circa 1930

28 inches. Velvet pads.

Value: Good $ 2,000
       Fair $ 1,400
       Poor $ 600

Mort and Evelyn Wood collection
Photo: Mort Wood

Maker unknown (Japan), Carnival pandas, circa 1920s

4½ inches. Celluloid head with Japan stamped on back. Cloth body. Sawdust stuffing. Hang cord protrudes from head. Painted eyes.

Value (each) :	Good	$	35
	Fair	$	25
	Poor	$	10

Michaud collection
Photo: T. Michaud

Maker unknown (Japan), souvenir, circa 1930

4 inches. Sparse gold mohair. Ears sewn into slots in head. Tiny yellow glass eyes. One-piece head and body. Wire-jointed limbs. Bear came with tiny bottle of Scotch whisky and a celluloid label attached to neck. Souvenir from Niagara Falls.

Value:	Good	$	300
	Fair	$	225
	Poor	$	100

Helen (Peggy) Williams collection
Photo: Peggy Williams

Maker and country of origin unknown, bandsman, circa 1925

24 inches. Uniforms on these unusual bears are part of the body, which allows the producer to use mohair for the head only. They are also referred to as soldiers.

Value: Good $ 500
       Fair $ 350
       Poor $ 150

Jo Nell Harkrider collection
Photo: Robert Buntz

Maker and country of origin unknown, circa 1925

18 inches. Brown mohair. Excelsior stuffing. Closely set shoe-button eyes. Shaved muzzle. End of paws curve upward. Straight legs with oval feet.

Value: Good $ 750
       Fair $ 525
       Poor $ 225

Helen (Peggy) Williams collection
Photo: Peggy Williams

Maker and country of origin unknown, circa 1920s

14 inches. Long lavender mohair (faded to gray). Pirate costume not original (added to offset missing ear and eye).

Value: Good $ 400
       Fair $ 275
       Poor $ 125

Don and Helene Marlowe collection
Photo: Don and Helene Marlowe

Maker and country of origin unknown, circa 1920s

6 inches. This early miniature teddy is every bit a lady. Dress is tattered but original. Hairpiece not original. Worn but lovable condition.

Value: Good $ 250
       Fair $ 175
       Poor $ 75

Michaud collection
Photo: T. Michaud

Additional Listings, not pictured

Joy Toys (Australia), circa 1930

16 inches. Long gold mohair. Paw pads tend to come to a point. Large orange/red glass eyes.

Value: Good $ 700
       Fair $ 500
       Poor $ 150

Maker unknown (Japan), clown bear circa 1930

16 inches. Right side of body, right arm and leg are green mohair. Left side is pink. Jointed. Wears a clown hat and a ruff on his neck. Small glass eyes in the typical orange/red color of the day.

Value: Good $ 1,000
       Fair $ 700
       Poor $ 250

Maker and country of origin unknown, circa 1925

20 inches. Bright-gold mohair. Fully jointed. Felt pads. Clear glass eyes with pupil.

Value: Good $ 500
       Fair $ 350
       Poor $ 100

Maker and country of origin unknown, bear on wheels, circa 1930

18 inches. Cinnamon wool plush fabric. Metal frame with stamped wheels and rubber covering.

Value: Good $ 400
       Fair $ 275
       Poor $ 100

Fernand Martin (France) mechanical bear, circa 1927

7 inches. Fabric covering over metal body with metal nose, feet and hands. Bear holds a broom and sweeps when wound.

Value: Good $ 800
       Fair $ 550
       Poor $ 200

1930-1940

Eduard Cramer, circa 1930s

7½ inches. Mohair with black stitched nose, red mouth. This charmer was called Bearkin and originally came with a trunk and wardrobe of clothing.

Value:	Good	$	750
	Fair	$	525
	Poor	$	225

Note: The bear complete with original wardrobe and trunk, in good condition, would be valued in the range of $1,500.

Eduard Cramer, circa 1930s

18 inches. Bearkin.

Value:	Good	$	1,500
	Fair	$	1,000
	Poor	$	450

Jo Nell Harkrider collection
Photo: Robert Buntz

Eduard Cramer, circa 1930s

16 inches. Long brown mohair. Black nose and claw stitching, red mouth stitching.

Value:	Good	$	2,200
	Fair	$	1,550
	Poor	$	650

Rare Bears collection
Photo: Karen Strickland

Maker unknown (possibly E. Cramer), circa 1930s

20 inches. Rust mohair with pale gold inset muzzle. Excelsior stuffing, clear glass eyes, three claws on foot and paw. Replaced wool felt pads.

Value: Good $ 600
      Fair $ 425
      Poor $ 175

Donna McPherson collection
Photo: Donna McPherson

Schuco, tumbling teddy, circa 1930s

Mohair head, felt outfit over formed metal. Keywind mechanism allows teddy to do somersaults.

Value: Good $ 1,200
      Fair $ 850
      Poor $ 350

Michaud collection
Photo: T. Michaud

Steiff, circa 1930s

14 inches. Light-tan mohair.

Value: Good $ 1,000
      Fair $ 700
      Poor $ 300

Delores Buntz collection
Photo: Robert Buntz

Maker unknown, circa 1930s

8½ inches. Tan mohair. Wearing tin pinback "Press Bizzy Bear," probably a news giveaway from the 1930s. Sweater not original.

Value: Good $ 300
Fair $ 225
Poor $ 100

Michaud collection
Photo: T. Michaud

Maker unknown, bear on all fours, circa 1930s

7½ inches long. Bear and wagon came as a unit.

Value: Good $ 350
Fair $ 250
Poor $ 100

Jo Nell Harkrider collection
Photo: Robert Buntz

Maker unknown, bear on all fours, circa 1930s

8 inches long, 5 inches high. Mohair.

Value: Good $ 475
Fair $ 325
Poor $ 150

Delores Buntz Collection
Photo: Robert Buntz

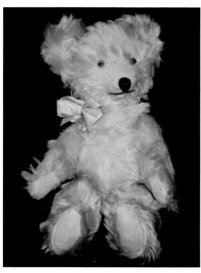

Knickerbocker, circa 1930s

12 inches. Bright-gold long mohair, amber glass eyes. Sheared-mohair long nose. Velvet pads.

Value: Good $ 350
       Fair $ 250
       Poor $ 100

Dolls and Bears of Charlton Court collection
Photo: Adrienne Zisser

Knickerbocker, circa 1930s

10 inches. Dark-apricot mohair, short legs, slightly curved arms. Felt pads, shaved pointy snout. Orange glass eyes.

Value: Good $ 300
       Fair $ 200
       Poor $ 75

Maker unknown, muff, circa 1930s

8 inches long. Light-blue plush, amber glass eyes.

Value: Good $ 200
       Fair $ 150
       Poor $ 50

Don and Helene Marlowe collection
Photo: Don and Helene Marlowe

Maker unknown, circa 1930s

25 inches. Black mohair (unusual color). Three pads replaced, one split open. Brown stitched nose.

Value: Good $ 500
Fair $ 350
Poor $ 150

Michaud collection
Photo: T. Michaud

Maker unknown, circa 1930s

15 inches. Cinnamon mohair, velveteen pads, low-set ears, shoe-button eyes.

Value: Good $ 250
Fair $ 175
Poor $ 75

Don and Helene Marlowe collection
Photo: Don and Helene Marlowe

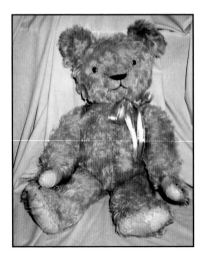

Maker unknown, musical teddy, circa 1930s

26 inches. Squeeze tummy to play music. Long curly bright mohair. Felt pads.

Value: Good $ 1,400
Fair $ 1,000
Poor $ 400

Dolls and Bears of Charlton Court collection
Photo: Adrienne Zisser

Maker unknown, bandsmen/soldier bears, circa 1930s

23-24 inches tall with hat. These teddies, sometimes produced in school colors, were popular with college students in the 1930s. Heads were mohair, rigid bodies were felt-covered, and legs were simply hollow tubes covered with felt pants. Glass eyes. Hats were trimmed in front with hemp. Inexpensively made.

Value:		
Good	$	400
Fair	$	275
Poor	$	125

Michaud collection
Photo: T. Michaud

Maker unknown, bear on wheels, circa 1930s

18 inches long, 11 inches high. Cotton plush fabric.

Value:		
Good	$	600
Fair	$	425
Poor	$	175

Jo Nell Harkrider collection
Photo: Robert Buntz

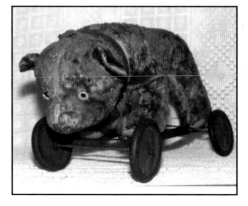

Chad Valley, circa 1930s

30 inches. White alpaca with beige kid leather on the inside of ears. Cotton pads. Embroidered nose and mouth. Football-shaped body. Well proportioned.

Value: Good $ 700
Fair $ 500
Poor $ 225

Donna McPherson collection
Photo: Donna McPherson

❖ Chad Valley bears are frequently labeled. If the label has a Royal Warrant printed on it, the bear was made after 1938, the year the company was awarded the warrant. Labels were typically sewn onto the foot pad, and even if the label has been removed, the outline can frequently still be seen.

Chiltern, pajama bag (night-dress case), circa 1930s

18 inches. Night dress cases in the form of dogs and cats were reasonably common in Great Britain in the 1930s to 1950s. Teddy bear cases were not as common, and are harder to find today.

Value: Good $ 400
Fair $ 275
Poor $ 125

Michaud Collection
Photo: T. Michaud

Chiltern, Hugmee, circa 1940

14 inches. Golden mohair, kapok stuffing, amber glass eyes.

Value: Good $ 450
       Fair $ 325
       Poor $ 125

Betty Smith collection
Photo: Donna McPherson

JK Farnell, circa 1930s

18 inches. Brown felt pads. Shoe-button eyes. Black felt under the gray embroidered nose.

Value: Good $ 2,000
       Fair $ 1,500
       Poor $ 500

Susan and Steve Swickard collection
Photo: T. Michaud

Alpha Farnell, pajama bag (night dress case), circa 1930s

15 inches. Wool fabric. Label on foot reads "Alpha Farnell Hygienic Soft Toy."

Value: Good $ 400
       Fair $ 275
       Poor $ 125

Michaud collection
Photo : T. Michaud

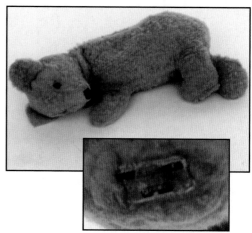

Left: Merrythought, Cheeky muff, circa 1930s

12 inches. Gold mohair head, acrylic body.

Value:

Good	$	300
Fair	$	200
Poor	$	100

Center & Right: Maker unknown (American), circa late 1930s

12 inches. Bear in center, white mohair. Bear on right, gold mohair. Unjointed, with tails. Glass eyes.

Value (each):

Good	$	150
Fair	$	100
Poor	$	50

Michaud collection
Photo: T. Michaud

Merrythought, circa 1930s

20 inches. Golden mohair, amber glass eyes. Head stuffed with excelsior, body with kapok. Brown embroidered nose. Three claws on feet and paws.

Value:

Good	$	300
Fair	$	225
Poor	$	100

Donna McPherson collection
Photo: Donna McPherson

JK Farnell, circa 1930s

18 inches. Long silky pale-gold mohair. Webbed stitched paws. Felt pads.

Value: Good $ 1,800
       Fair $ 1,250
       Poor $ 550

Dolls and Bears of Charlton Court collection
Photo: Adrienne Zisser

Merrythought, circa 1930s

15 inches

Value: Good $ 400
       Fair $ 275
       Poor $ 125

Jo Nell Harkrider collection
Photo: Robert Buntz

Dean's, polar bear, circa 1930s

17 inches. White mohair. Unjointed. Metal ID button in bottom of foot.

Value: Good $ 450
       Fair $ 325
       Poor $ 125

Maker unknown (United States), circa 1935

22 inches. Wool/mohair blend. Glass eyes. Collar not original.

Value: Good $ 300
       Fair $ 225
       Poor $ 100

Michaud collection
Photo: T. Michaud

Maker unknown, (possibly Dean's), circa 1930s

18 inches. Large head and short arms are disc-jointed. Legs are unjointed, in sitting position.

Value: Good $ 600
       Fair $ 425
       Poor $ 175

Jo Nell Harkrider collection
Photo: Robert Buntz

Merrythought, circa 1932

This teddy has a coat of art silk, a man-made material meant to replace mohair. It was not widely accepted and was used for a short time period. The bear is one of the Magnet bear series. Unusual red color. Foot label. Excellent condition. Rare.

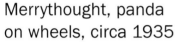

Value: Good $ 1,800
      Fair $ 1,250
      Poor $ 550

Donna McPherson collection
Photo: Donna McPherson

Merrythought, panda on wheels, circa 1935

12 inches. Merrythought label on back of carriage, also on foot of panda. This British firm was one of the first to produce pandas.

Value: Good $ 750
      Fair $ 550
      Poor $ 200

Michaud collection
Photo: T. Michaud

Maker unknown (possibly Chiltern or Twyford), circa 1930s

12 inches. Gold mohair, amber glass eyes, worn rexine pads. Stubby feet.

Value:	Good	$	250
	Fair	$	175
	Poor	$	75

Don and Helene Marlowe collection
Photo: Don and Helene Marlowe

Maker unknown, circa 1930s

20 inches. Off-white mohair. Glasses and trim not original. Head has excelsior stuffing; body and limbs have kapok stuffing.

Value:	Good	$	450
	Fair	$	325
	Poor	$	125

Michaud collection
Photo: T. Michaud

Maker unknown, circa 1930s

20 inches. Mohair. Large ears give this teddy great appeal.

Value:	Good	$	400
	Fair	$	275
	Poor	$	125

Jo Nell Harkrider collection
Photo: Robert Buntz

Maker unknown (possibly Chad Valley), circa 1930s

8 inches. Light-gold mohair, short pointed curved arms, pointed feet. Amber glass eyes, worn velveteen pads.

Value: Good $ 350
Fair $ 250
Poor $ 100

Don and Helene Marlowe collection
Photo: Don and Helene Marlowe

Maker unknown, circa 1930s

17 inches. Rust-brown mohair. Paw pads replaced. Great character.

Value: Good $ 400
Fair $ 275
Poor $ 125

Maker and country of origin unknown, circa 1930s

23 inches. Long rust mohair. Felt paw and foot pads. Some wear at mouth. Charming face.

Value: Good $ 400
Fair $ 275
Poor $ 125

Michaud collection
Photo: T. Michaud

Maker unknown, circa 1930s

16 inches. Mohair.

Value: Good $ 450
        Fair $ 325
        Poor $ 125

Delores Buntz collection
Photo: Robert Buntz

Maker unknown, circa 1930s

12 inches. Mohair with cotton pads.
Glasses not original.

Value: Good $ 450
        Fair $ 325
        Poor $ 125

Teddy's friend is a 13-inch Raggedy Ann two-face doll (sleeping face on back of head) by the Georgene Novelty Co., circa 1940s.

Susan and Steve Swickard collection
Photo: T. Michaud

Additional Listings, not pictured

Chiltern, circa 1930

20 inches. Jointed.

Value: Good $ 700
       Fair $ 500
       Poor $ 200

Chiltern, circa 1930

14 inches. Brown mohair. Jointed

Value: Good $ 600
       Fair $ 425
       Poor $ 175

Chad Valley, circa 1931

18 inches. Pale-gold mohair. Kapok stuffing. Metal button in ear reads "Chad Valley. British Hygienic Toys." Label on left foot pad.

Value: Good $ 1,000
       Fair $ 700
       Poor $ 300

Dean's, circa 1932

15 inches. Light-gold mohair. Excelsior stuffing in head; kapok stuffing in body.

Value: Good $ 600
       Fair $ 400
       Poor $ 150

Maker unknown (Holland), circa 1930s

16 inches. Brown mohair with inset muzzle and ear fronts. External rod joints.

Value:
Good	$	400
Fair	$	275
Poor	$	125

Delores Buntz collection
Photo: Robert Buntz

Maker unknown (France), circa 1930s

10 inches. This bear has pin or rod joints that cause both legs (or arms) to move when just one limb is moved. This type of joint is more typically found in Japanese and American bears of that era.

Value:
Good	$	200
Fair	$	150
Poor	$	50

Jo Nell Harkrider collection
Photo: Robert Buntz

Maker unknown (France), circa 1930s

15 inches. Light-blond silky mohair, clear glass eyes. Light peach felt pads. Straw stuffing. Open red felt mouth.

Value:
Good	$	500
Fair	$	350
Poor	$	150

Dolls and Bears of Charlton Court collection
Photo: Adrienne Zisser

Herman Pecker (Japan), circa 1930s

7½ inches. Pink cotton fabric. Original paper tag attached to chain. Plastic collar with steel bell. Probably a carnival bear.

Value: Good $ 150
with original tag $ 200
Fair $ 100
Poor $ 25

Michaud collection
Photo: T. Michaud

Maker unknown (Japan), carnival bear, circa 1930s

6½ inches. Wire-jointed limbs. Rayon covering. Glass eyes.

Value: Good $ 75
Fair $ 50
Poor $ 25

Michaud collection
Photo: T. Michaud

Maker and country of origin unknown, mechanical polar bear, circa 1930s

9½ inches long. Art silk fabric. When the tail is twisted, the head moves in a circular motion. Some soiling. Rare.

Value: Good $ 750
Fair $ 525
Poor $ 225

Michaud collection
Photo: T. Michaud

Maker and country of origin unknown, miniature, circa 1930s

4 inches. Gold mohair. Older miniature teddies are difficult to find.

Value:	Good	$	200
	Fair	$	150
	Poor	$	50

Michaud Collection
Photo: T. Michaud

Maker and country of origin unknown, miniature, circa 1930s

3¾ inches. Mohair. Excessive wear. Knit sweater old, but probably not original.

Value:	Good	$	200
	Fair	$	150
	Poor	$	50

Michaud collection
Photo: T. Michaud

Maker and country of origin unknown, panda, circa 1937

16 inches. Dated by original owner. Well-loved and worn cotton plush, hard stuffed body, short arms, stubby feet, cone-shaped head with pointed nose. Eyes missing.

Value:	Good	$	250
	Fair	$	175
	Poor	$	75

Don and Helene Marlowe collection
Photo: Don and Helene Marlowe

1940-1950

Clemens, circa 1948

20 inches. This German manufacturer began making bears in 1947; they are in strong demand worldwide.

Value:	Good	$	600
	Fair	$	425
	Poor	$	175

Jo Nell Harkrider collection
Photo: Robert Buntz

Schuco, yes/no Tricky bear, circa 1950

13 inches. Beige mohair. Excelsior stuffing. Arms turn in and downward at the wrist. Oval felt pads with cardboard insert on feet. Yes/no mechanism operated by tail.

Value:	Good	$	600
	Fair	$	425
	Poor	$	175

Helen (Peggy) Williams collection
Photo: Peggy Williams

Steiff, musical bear, circa 1950
15 inches

Value:	Good	$	2,200
	Fair	$	1,550
	Poor	$	650

Linda Mullins Collection
Photo: Linda Mullins

❖Most of the yes/no movement bears were made by Schuco. Steiff and a few other makers also made a smaller number.

Back: **Maker unknown (East Germany), three bears set, circa 1945-50**

2 to 6 inches. In original box. Rare.

Value: Good $ 200
      Fair $ 150
      Poor $ 75

Front: **Maker unknown (West Germany), pull toy, circa 1945-50**

Bears spin in a circle as toy is pulled.

Value: Good $ 200
      Fair $ 150
      Poor $ 75

Jo Nell Harkrider collection
Photo: Robert Buntz

Maker unknown, circa 1940s

22 inches. Cream wool fabric, excelsior stuffing, amber glass eyes. Metal nose. Open mouth of red wool felt.

Value: Good $ 200
      Fair $ 150
      Poor $ 75

Donna McPherson collection
Photo: Donna McPherson

❖The German teddy bear makers were anxious to return to their trade following World War II. During the early post war years many new companies got their start, including such recognizable names as Grisley, Petz, Althans and Clemens. Some of the founders of these companies had roots in the business as employees of older firms. There was an acute shortage of plush fabric to produce bears, and some of the more enterprising companies used surplus materials, such as army blankets to produce teddies. Herta Girz, one of the new firms, operating under the trade name Hegi, managed to get a sub contract with Schuco to produce the famous Biggo Bello series for them. Your Biggo Bello bear or character may carry a Schuco label, but we now know it was actually produced by a little known German company called Hegi.

Maker unknown (East Germany), miniature, circa 1945-50

3 inches. Brown mohair. Paper label on foot indicates this bear was made in East Germany. Rare with label.

Value:			
Good	$	150
Fair	$	100
Poor	$	50

Michaud collection
Photo: T. Michaud

Maker unknown (East Germany), circa 1945-50

19 inches. Tipped mohair, excelsior stuffing. Inner ears are shaved mohair. Open mouth of red wool felt. Short arms.

Value:			
Good	$	500
Fair	$	350
Poor	$	150

Donna McPherson collection
Photo: Donna McPherson

Maker unknown (East Germany), circa 1945-50

7 and 10 inches. These hard-to-find teddies are short-nap gold mohair, with pin-jointed arms and legs. The heads are not jointed. Both have their original paper labels marked "East Germany." The label is seldom found with the bears, and they are occasionally attributed to a Japanese maker because of their construction.

Value (either size):			
Good	$	150
Fair	$	100
Poor	$	50

Susan and Steve Swickard collection
Photo: T. Michaud

Character, circa 1940-50

Large bear, 24 inches. Dense white woolly plush, large red glass eyes, felt pads with air brushed claws. Cloth ID tag on left ear.

Value: Good $ 300
      Fair $ 200
      Poor $ 100

Small bear, 11 inches. Gold mohair, felt pads, amber glass eyes. Cloth ID tag on left ear.

Value: Good $ 150
      Fair $ 100
      Poor $ 50

Don and Helene Marlowe collection
Photo: Don and Helene Marlowe

Knickerbocker, circa 1940s

20 inches. Light-tan mohair, velveteen inset snout, large ears with velveteen lining, velveteen paw pads. Unusual clear glass eyes painted green on back.

Value: Good $ 450
      Fair $ 325
      Poor $ 125

Don and Helene Marlowe collection
Photo: Don and Helene Marlowe

Knickerbocker, circa 1940s

21 inches. Typical cinnamon mohair, felt pads, shaved snout. Amber glass eyes.

Value: Good $ 450
      Fair $ 325
      Poor $ 125

Don and Helen Marlowe collection
Photo: Don and Helene Marlowe

Maker unknown, circa 1940s

14 inches. Dark-brown silky plush, velveteen pads, cardboard insoles in feet. Amber glass eyes. Large ears. Sweater and scarf not original.

Value:	Good	$	250
	Fair	$	175
	Poor	$	75

Don and Helene Marlowe collection
Photo: Don and Helene Marlowe

Maker unknown, panda, circa 1940s

25 inches. Hard stuffed body with synthetic black-and-white plush. Working squeaker. Cotton paw pads. Red embroidered tongue. Eyes missing.

Value:	Good	$	350
	Fair	$	250
	Poor	$	100

Maker unknown (Japan), circa 1950s

9 inches. Acrylic plush. Inset snout, airbrushed velvet pads, amber glass eyes.

Value:	Good	$	150
	Fair	$	100
	Poor	$	50

Don and Helene Marlowe collection
Photo: Don and Helene Marlowe

Knickerbocker, circa 1940s

Large (seated) bear, 16 inches. Dark-brown mohair, velveteen pads, large ears, amber glass eyes. Inset shaved snout.

Value: Good $ 400
       Fair $ 275
       Poor $ 125

Small (standing) bear 12 inches. Long cinnamon mohair, short curved arms, felt pads, glass eyes. Inset shaved snout.

Value: Good $ 300
       Fair $ 200
       Poor $ 100

Don and Helene Marlowe collection
Photo: Don and Helene Marlowe

Maker unknown, carnival-style collegiate bear, circa 1940s

12½ inches. Black and gold wool. Celluloid "googly" eyes. These bears were produced in a variety of school colors.

Value: Good $ 75
       Fair $ 50
       Poor $ 25

Michaud collection
Photo: T. Michaud

Knickerbocker, circa 1940s

17½ inches. White mohair. Unusual design with ear front and head side cut from same piece of mohair.

Value: Good $ 325
       Fair $ 225
       Poor $ 100

Michaud collection
Photo: T. Michaud

Wendy Boston, circa 1945-50

6 inches seated. Unjointed. This firm started producing bears after World War II, and quickly captured a large share of the British teddy market. They remain a favorite of arctophiles today. Original label on back of left leg. Plush fabric.

Value:	Good	$	200
	Fair	$	150
	Poor	$	50

Susan and Steve Swickard collection
Photo: T. Michaud

Wendy Boston, circa 1945-50

14½ inches. Unjointed. Made in South Wales. Label on foot reads: "A Play Safe Toy Made in Great Britain by Wendy Boston."

Value:	Good	$	200
	Fair	$	150
	Poor	$	50

Michaud collection
Photo: T. Michaud

BeBe Dolls, circa 1942

12 inches. Mohair. Purchased in London, England with leg pulled off. When we opened bear to repair it, we discovered a note from a Miss Edna Farr, age 17, giving her address. Subsequent investigation by Gerry Grey led to the discovery of this doll and bear firm that produced these toys during the war years. The late Miss Edna was 17 years of age in 1942 and put the note inside the bear while working at the factory. Condition excellent (after repair to leg).

Value:	Good	$	400
With provenance		$	800
	Fair	$	250
	Poor	$	100

Michaud collection
Photo: T. Michaud

Chiltern Hugmee, circa 1940s

14 inches. Pale-gold mohair, kapok stuffing. Amber glass eyes, velvet pads.

Value: Good $ 450
       Fair $ 325
       Poor $ 125

Donna McPherson collection
Photo: Donna McPherson

Merrythought, circa 1940s

14 inches. Gold medium-length mohair. Red foot and paw pads with Merrythought label on left foot. Claws in style unique to this British firm.

Value: Good $ 1,000
       Fair $ 700
       Poor $ 300

Rare Bears collection
Photo: Karen Strickland

Merrythought, Punkinhead, circa 1950s

13 inches. In need of restoration, this rare example is in blue, white and gold mohair. He has wool felt pads, excelsior stuffing, velvet muzzle and feet. He still retains his label.

Value: Good $ 1,500
        Fair $ 1,000
        Poor $ 600

Donna McPherson collection
Photo: Donna McPherson

Maker unknown, circa 1940s

16 inches. Blond mohair, short arms and legs, worn rexine pads, amber glass eyes. Sweater not original.

Value: Good $ 300
        Fair $ 200
        Poor $ 100

Don and Helene Marlowe collection
Photo: Don and Helene Marlowe

Merrythought, panda, circa 1940s

24 inches. Art silk fabric. Orange glass eyes. Stuffed with excelsior. Red rexine paw and foot pads. Working growler.

Value: Good $ 400
       Fair $ 275
       Poor $ 125

Donna McPherson collection
Photo: Donna McPherson

Merrythought, Punkinhead, circa 1950

10 inches. Mohair. Velvet muzzle and feet. Glass eyes. This example is missing the original pants.

Value: Good $ 800
       Fair $ 550
       Poor $ 250

Donna McPherson collection
Photo: Donna McPherson

Berg (Austria), circa 1950

30 inches. Red metal Berg heart on chest.

Value: Good $ 1,000
        Fair $ 700
        Poor $ 300

Mort and Evelyn Wood collection
Photo: Mort Wood

❖ If your teddy has a small brass button on his chest just below the neckline, it might be a trademark of the French bear firm M. Pintel Fils dating from the 1920s. Most of their bears were of lesser quality than those made in Germany, utilizing short-nap mohair or rayon plush.

M. Pintel-Fils (France), circa 1940s

22 inches. Light-pink mohair with contrasting beige mohair pads and ear inserts. No button. Hard to find.

Value: Good $ 450
        Fair $ 325
        Poor $ 125

Michaud collection
Photo: T. Michaud

Maker unknown (Australia), koala muff, circa 1940s

8 inches long, 6 inches high. This unusual muff was actually made of real Kangaroo hide before the practice was outlawed.

Value: Good $ 100
      Fair $ 75
      Poor $ 30

Michaud collection
Photo: T. Michaud

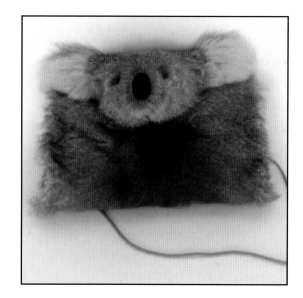

Maker unknown (Japan), carnival-type bear, circa 1950

14 inches. Rayon plush.

Value: Good $ 200
      Fair $ 150
      Poor $ 75

Jo Nell Harkrider collection
Photo: Robert Buntz

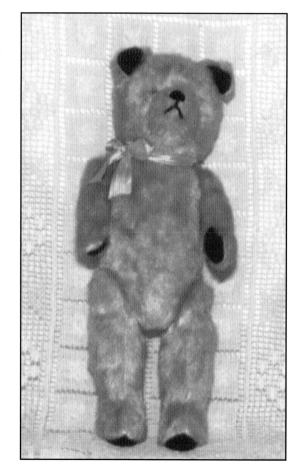

Additional Listing, not pictured

Tara (Ireland), circa 1940s

22 inches. Light tan mohair. Brown felt pads. Glass eyes.

Value:	Good	$	450
	Fair	$	325
	Poor	$	125

Maker unknown (France), circa 1948

20 inches. Beige mohair. Fully jointed. Kapok stuffing.

Value:	Good	$	500
	Fair	$	350
	Poor	$	100

FADAP (France), circa 1946

19 inches. Short-nap pale-gold mohair. Large cupped ears. No markings.

Value:	Good	$	600
	Fair	$	400
	Poor	$	175

Joy Toys (Australia), circa 1947

26 inches. Head is not jointed. Nose stitching is distinguished by ends sweeping up. Oil-cloth paw pads tend to come to a point. Label on foot.

Value:	Good	$	400
	Fair	$	275
	Poor	$	100

Alps (Japan), battery-operated drinking panda, circa 1948-1950

9 ½ inches. Bear is seated on a metal log. When operated, he pours a drink from a bottle into a cup, then drinks. The post-war years were the heyday of the Japanese battery-operated toys and they are avidly sought by collectors today. Note: if they are not in working condition, the value drops dramatically.

Value:	Good	$	250
	Fair (working)	$	150
	Poor (not working)	$	40

Pedigree (Ireland), circa 1945

29 inches. Glass eyes. Gold mohair with chocolate-colored velvet pads. Kapok stuffed. Tag on back of neck reads "Pedigree — made in Ireland."

Value:	Good	$	800
	Fair	$	550
	Poor	$	200

1950-1960

Hermann, circa 1950s

20 inches. Pale-brown mohair. Short-nap mohair inset snout. Reddish-gold eyes with black center. Felt paw and foot pads.

Value:	Good	$	350
	Fair	$	250
	Poor	$	100

Rare Bears collection
Photo: Karen Strickland

Maker unknown, circa 1950s

4 inches. Unusual big feet, similar in style to Steiff Dickie bears. Hole in left foot pad has been mended.

Value:	Good	$	175
	Fair	$	125
	Poor	$	50

Michaud collection
Photo: T. Michaud

Schuco, miniature panda, circa 1950s

3½ inches. The panda is one of the hardest to find and most desirable of the Schuco miniatures. Mohair.

Value:	Good	$	250
	Fair	$	175
	Poor	$	75

Michaud collection
Photo: T. Michaud

Steiff, polar bear, circa 1950s

8 inches. Bear stands on all fours. Blue glass eyes, off-white mohair. Felt pads, stitched claws.

Value:			
	Good	$	250
	Fair	$	175
	Poor	$	75

Dolls and Bears of Charlton Court collection
Photo: Adrienne Zisser

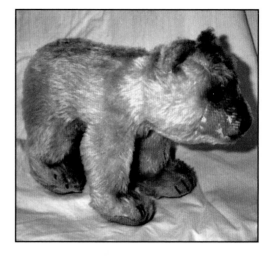

Steiff, circa 1950s

14 inches. White mohair. Chest tag reads "original teddy."

Value:			
	Good	$	900
	Fair	$	650
	Poor	$	250

Rare Bears collection
Photo: Karen Strickland

Steiff, Zotty, circa 1950s

12 inches. This popular style of open-mouth bear was also produced by several other firms, including Hermann.

Value:			
	Good	$	175
	Fair	$	125
	Poor	$	50

Delores Buntz Collection
Photo: Robert Buntz

Schuco, Rolly bear, circa 1950s

8 inches. Mechanical bear with key wind motor skates on roller blades.

Value: Good $ 1,500
Fair $ 1,000
Poor $ 500

Jo Nell Harkrider collection
Photo: Robert Buntz

Left: Schuco, Tricky yes/no bear, circa 1950s

12 inches. A highly sought-after bear with a great face.

Value: Good $ 2,000
Fair $ 1,400
Poor $ 600

Right: Schuco, yes/no bear, circa 1950s

10 inches. Although Schuco produced the yes/no bears in large quantities, they are still very much in demand and not that easy to find.

Value: Good $ 1,000
Fair $ 700
Poor $ 300

Sue Pearson collection
Photo: Sue Pearson

Steiff, circa 1950s

30 inches. Dense, long, curly champagne-colored mohair. Felt paw pads. Original ribbon on neck.

Value: Good $ 4,800
Fair $ 3,350
Poor $ 1,450

Dolls and Bears of Charlton Court collection
Photo: Adrienne Zisser

Steiff, panda, circa 1950s

6 inches

Value: Good $ 700
       Fair $ 500
       Poor $ 200

Jo Nell Harkrider collectoin
Photo: Robert Buntz

Steiff, koalas, circa 1950s

12 inches (mother), 5 inches (baby). Koalas are technically not teddy bears, but are frequently found in teddy collections and are prized by many arctophiles.

Value (12 inch):   Good $ 1,200
                Fair $ 850
                Poor $ 350

Value (5 inch):   Good $ 500
               Fair $ 350
               Poor $ 150

Jo Nell Harkrider collection
Photo: Robert Buntz

Additional Listings, not pictured

Jopi, circa 1950s

16 inches. Long gold mohair with red tipping. Excelsior stuffing. Glass eyes. Musical.

Value: Good $ 3,000
        Fair $ 2,200
        Poor $ 750

Schuco Rolly Bear, circa 1950s

8 ½ inches. Mohair over metal body. Bear is on roller skates and carries a walking stick. Windup mechanism.

Value: Good $1,800 (in original box)
        Fair $1,200
        Poor $ 500

Steiff, Zotty, circa 1959

8½ inches. Light-caramel mohair with white chest and snout. Note: the open-mouth Zotty was produced by Steiff over a wide range of years and in a wide range of sizes. A similar bear was produced by Hermann, as well as by other manufacturers. It is difficult to tell them apart unless the bear has tags and/or a button in ear.

Value: Good $ 350
        Fair $ 250
        Poor $ 100

Gund, circa 1950s

34 inches. Unusually large unjointed bear. Rust plush fabric. Label on side reads "A Gund creation – J. Swedlin Inc., Brooklyn NY. "

Value: Good $ 150
Fair $ 100
Poor $ 50

Susan and Steve Swickard collection
Photo: T. Michaud

Knickerbocker, Teddy Kuddles, circa 1950s

14 inches. Light-blond silky plush, soft stuffing, jointed head, large ears. Cloth ID tag on tummy.

Value: Good $ 100
Fair $ 75
Poor $ 35

Don and Helene Marlowe collection
Photo: Don and Helene Marlowe

Knickerbocker, circa 1950s

11 inches. Dark-brown mohair, velvet insert muzzle and ear fronts. Head has excelsior stuffing; body has kapok stuffing.

Value: Good $ 250
Fair $ 175
Poor $ 75

Donna McPherson collection
Photo: Donna McPherson

Knickerbocker, circa 1950s

15½ inches. Cinnamon medium-length mohair. Velour pads and inset snout.

Value: Good $ 250
       Fair $ 175
       Poor $ 75

Rare Bears collection
Photo: Karen Strickland

Knickerbocker, circa 1950s

16 inches. Yellow-gold mohair with center-seam ID. Large dish ears.

Value: Good $ 225
       Fair $ 150
       Poor $ 50

Rare Bears collection
Photo: Karen Strickland

Maker unknown, electric-eye bear, circa 1950s

11 inches. While most electric-eye bears were a product of the 1920s and 1930s, an unknown maker revived the novelty in the 1950s. Bear has synthetic plush, red felt tongue and tiny light-bulb eyes. An opening in the back allows for access to batteries. Unjointed.

Value: Good $ 100
       Fair $ 75
       Poor $ 35

Don and Helene Marlowe collection
Photo: Don and Helene Marlowe

Maker unknown, panda, circa 1950s

21 inches. This carnival-type panda is unjointed and has the original hang tag that reads "I-M-A Sil-Bear. Fred Silber Co. Ferndale, Mich." It is assumed that Silber was the distributor and the bear was likely mass-produced offshore.

Value: Good $ 75
       Fair $ 50
       Poor $ 25

Michaud collection
Photo: T. Michaud

Maker unknown (imported), Smokey Bear circa 1950s

14 inches. First in a series of Smokey Bears that are still made today. The first Smokey had an all-vinyl head. He was followed by a second series with vinyl face and plush head, then by a model with an all-plush head. Cotton plush. This bear is wearing several Smokey Bear pins. Original bear came with shovel.

Value: Good (complete) $ 350
        Fair $ 250
        Poor $ 100

Michaud collection
Photo: T. Michaud

Chad Valley, circa 1950s

11½ inches. Gold mohair. Rexine pads. Kapok stuffing.

Value:			
	Good	$	350
	Fair	$	250
	Poor	$	100

Michaud collection
Photo: T. Michaud

Chad Valley, Sooty, circa 1950s

12 inches. Sooty was a popular British cartoon and TV character and his "trade mark" design is black ears on gold mohair.

Value:			
	Good	$	150
	Fair	$	100
	Poor	$	50

Delores Buntz collection
Photo: Robert Buntz

Left: Chad Valley, circa 1950s

16 inches. Original foot label and chest tag--an unusual find.

Value:			
	Good	$	600
	Fair	$	425
	Poor	$	175

Right: Chad Valley, circa 1950s

14 inches. Foot label.

Value:			
	Good	$	500
	Fair	$	350
	Poor	$	150

Sue Pearson collection
Photo: Sue Pearson

Merrythought, circa 1950s

13 inches. Gold mohair, dark-brown soft cloth pads. Traces of stitching from original label. Large music box inside (not working).

Value: Good $ 400
   Fair $ 275
   Poor $ 125

Donna McPherson collection
Photo: Donna McPherson

Left: Merrythought, Cheeky, circa 1960

14 inches. Label on right foot. Inset muzzle.

Value: Good $ 750
    Fair $ 525
    Poor $ 225

Right: Merrythought, Cheeky, circa 1960

12 inches. Mohair slightly worn.

Value: Good $ 600
    Fair $ 425
    Poor $ 175

Sue Pearson collection
Photo: Sue Pearson

❖If your teddy has a Merrythought label on his foot that includes the wording "Ironbridge, Shrops," he dates from after 1957 when these words were added to their labels.

Left: Merrythought, circa 1950s

21 inches. Bear is in good condition and still retains the label.

Value: Good $ 750
Fair $ 525
Poor $ 225

Right: Chiltern, Tingaling Bruin, circa 1953

12 inches. This musical teddy derives his name from a simple musical sound that is made when simply tilting the bear back and forth. Short body, small ears set wide apart, large feet.

Value: Good $ 650
Fair $ 450
Poor $ 200

Sue Pearson collection
Photo: Sue Pearson

Chiltern Hugmee, circa 1950s

19 inches. Mohair slightly worn. Antique dress.

Value: Good $ 600
Fair $ 425
Poor $ 175

Sue Pearson collection
Photo: Sue Pearson

Chiltern, Hugmee, circa 1950s

14 inches. Golden plush mohair, kapok stuffing in body and legs, excelsior stuffing in head (typical of British bears of this era). Reddish-brown glass eyes. Short chubby body, short thick legs with pointed feet.

Value:	Good	$	500
	Fair	$	350
	Poor	$	150

Helen (Peggy) Williams collection
Photo: Peggy Williams

Chiltern, circa 1950s

12 inches. Mohair. This bear collects pins in his adventures and is obviously well-traveled.

Value:	Good	$	250
	Fair	$	175
	Poor	$	100

Delores Buntz collection
Photo: Robert Buntz

Chiltern, circa 1960

11 inches. Alpaca fabric, kapok stuffing, rexine pads. Brown glass eyes.

Value: Good $ 200
Fair $ 150
Poor $ 75

Keith Clark collection
Photo: Donna McPherson

Twyford, circa 1950s

16 inches. Beautiful cinnamon medium-length mohair. Felt paw and foot pads. Great face.

Value: Good $ 375
Fair $ 250
Poor $ 100

Rare Bears collection
Photo: Karen Strickland

Twyford, circa 1950s

31 inches. Short cinnamon mohair. ID in side seam. A great example of this popular British firm's bears.

Value: Good $ 950
       Fair $ 650
       Poor $ 275

Rare Bears collection
Photo: Karen Strickland

Twyford, circa 1950s

12 inches. White mohair, red paw and foot pads. Reddish-gold eyes with black center.

Value: Good $ 300
       Fair $ 200
       Poor $ 100

Rare Bears collection
Photo: Karen Strickland

Efray, circa 1950s

13 inches. Alpaca. Kapok stuffing. Plastic safety eyes. Short limbs and feet. Brown velvet pads.

Value: Good $ 250
Fair $ 175
Poor $ 75

Donna McPherson collection
Photo: Donna McPherson

Maker unknown, circa 1950s

12 inches. Pale-gold mohair, kapok stuffing, white rayon muzzle insert. Velvet paws. Cardboard discs in feet.

Value: Good $ 200
Fair $ 150
Poor $ 75

Donna McPherson collection
Photo: Donna McPherson

Left: Maker unknown, circa 1950s

16 inches. This charmer is an unusual pink mohair, an uncommon color for this era.

Value: Good $ 350
        Fair $ 250
        Poor $ 100

Additional Listings, not pictured

Chiltern, circa 1950s

20 inches. Mohair.

Value: Good $ 275
        Fair $ 200
        Poor $ 75

Chad Valley, circa 1950s

11 inches. Mohair with velour pads. Plastic eyes. Label on left side seam.

Value: Good $ 200
        Fair $ 140
        Poor $ 60

Chad Valley, circa 1950s

14 inches. Mohair. With label.

Value: Good $ 350
        Fair $ 250
        Poor $ 100

Right: Dean's, circa 1930s

15 inches. This is a great example of a bear produced by the oldest firm in Britain still producing teddy bears.

Value: Good $ 1,000
        Fair $ 700
        Poor $ 300

Sue Pearson collection
Photo: Sue Pearson

Chad Valley, circa 1950s

28 inches. Short-nap gold mohair. Foot label on right foot pad. Unusual size.

Value: Good $ 850
        Fair $ 600
        Poor $ 250

Maker unknown, circa 1950s

17 inches. Blue mohair

Value: Good $ 425
        Fair $ 300
        Poor $ 125

Marelis (Australia), koala, circa 1950s

4 inches. This toy is made from kangaroo hide, a practice now outlawed. It carries the original paper label and is called a Blue Gum Baby, after the Australian cartoon character Billy Blue Gum. The label also says "Marelis product, Sydney."

Value: Good $ 75
        Fair $ 50
        Poor $ 25

Michaud collection
Photo: T. Michaud

FADAP (France), circa 1950s

15 inches. Bear wears an antique silk jacket to cover his well-loved condition.

Value: Good $ 500
        Fair $ 350
        Poor $ 150

Sue Pearson collection
Photo: Sue Pearson

Pedigree (Ireland), circa 1950s

10 inches. Unusual head design uses four pieces with no gusset.

Value: Good $ 275
        Fair $ 175
        Poor $ 75

Michaud collection
Photo: T. Michaud

Tara (Ireland), circa 1950s

24 inches. Black-and-white mohair.
Large orange-and-black plastic eyes
(unique to this company). ID says
"Made in the Republic of Ireland."
Hard to find.

Value:	Good	$	850
	Fair	$	600
	Poor	$	250

Rare Bears collection
Photo: Karen Strickland

Maker unknown (Japan), bear on all fours, circa 1950s

4 inches long, 3 inches high.

Value:	Good	$	200
	Fair	$	150
	Poor	$	75

Delores Buntz collection
Photo: Robert Buntz

Maker unknown (Japan), circa 1950s

10 inches. Shiny nylon plush.
Excelsior stuffing. Small ears tucked
into holes on head seam. Gold plastic eyes with black centers. Short
arms and legs with no pads. Large
head with short body.

Value:	Good	$	200
	Fair	$	150
	Poor	$	60

Helen (Peggy) Williams collection
Photo: Peggy Williams

Maker and country of origin unknown, circa 1950s

Musical bear. Head moves when music plays. 16 inches. Tan short mohair, glass eyes. Felt paw pads (pointed at top).

Value: Good $ 350
       Fair $ 250
       Poor $ 100

Dolls and Bears of Charlton Court collection
Photo: Adrienne Zisser

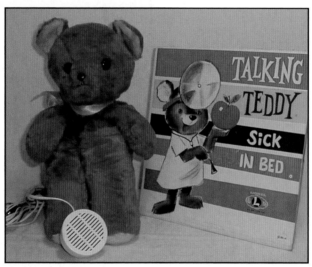

Maker and country of origin unknown, Talking Teddy, circa 1959-61

17½ inches. Bear came with a suitcase record player and a 33.3 long-play recording that played through a voice box in teddy. This unique set is owned by Susan and Steve Swickard and was Susan's bear as a child. It inspired the name of their teddy bear specialty shop, "The Talking Teddy" in Estes Park, Colorado.

Value: Good (complete) $ 250
        Fair $ 175
        Poor $ 75

Susan and Steve Swickard collection
Photo: T. Michaud

1960-1970

Hermann, Zotty-type open mouth, circa 1960s

Back row: 16 inches
Center row, left to right: 8, 10, 12 inches
Front row: 12-inch floppy. Identified by their yarn nose stitching that extends down each side of nose.

Value:	Good	$ 100-$350
	Fair	$ 75-$250
	Poor	$ 30-$100

Dolls and Bears of Charlton Court collection
Photo: Adrienne Zisser

Schuco, Bigo Bello Pooh, circa 1960s

10 inches. Gold short-nap mohair. Two unique designs in this bear; he has "flex limbs," meaning that instead of having normal joints, his arms can be posed in a variety of positions. He also has what is believed to be a plastic "mask" under the face to allow consistent shaping. Original hang tag.

Value:	Good	$ 2,500 (with tag)
	Fair	$ 1,750
	Poor	$ 750

Michaud collection
Photo : T. Michaud

Steiff, Cosy teddy, circa 1968

12 inches

Value:	Good	$ 550
	Fair	$ 375
	Poor	$ 175

Jo Nell Harkrider collection
Photo: Robert Buntz

Top: Steiff Clifford
Berryman bear™,
circa 1987

14 inches

Value: Good $ 300
      Fair $ 200
      Poor $ 75

Bottom: **Steiff, studio bear
on all fours, circa 1970**
66 inches. The studio animals were
meant for store displays.

Value: Good $ 6,500
      Fair $ 4,500
      Poor $ 1,950

Linda Mullins Collection
Photo: Linda Mullins

Maker unknown,
circa 1960s

15 inches. Beige mohair, shaved
muzzle and pads of mohair. Plastic
eyes.

Value: Good $ 200
      Fair $ 150
      Poor $ 50

Donna McPherson collection
Photo: Donna McPherson

Left: Chiltern, Hugmee, circa 1960s

14 inches. All original.

Value:	Good	$	475
	Fair	$	325
	Poor	$	150

Right: Chiltern, Hugmee, circa 1960s

24 inches. All original.

Value:	Good	$	750
	Fair	$	525
	Poor	$	225

Sue Pearson collection
Photo: Sue Pearson

Left: Merrythought, Cheeky, circa 1960

9 inches. Good condition with foot label.

Value:	Good	$	650
	Fair	$	450
	Poor	$	200

Right: Merrythought Cheeky, circa 1960s

13 inches. Good condition. Foot label.

Value:	Good	$	750
	Fair	$	525
	Poor	$	225

Sue Pearson collection
Photo: Sue Pearson

Left: Merrythought, circa 1960s

15 inches. Label on foot.

Value: Good $ 600
      Fair $ 425
      Poor $ 175

Center: Chad Valley, circa 1960s

16 inches. Label on foot.

Value: Good $ 450
      Fair $ 325
      Poor $ 125

Right: Maker unknown, circa 1930s

14 inches. Great face.

Value: Good $ 475
      Fair $ 325
      Poor $ 150

Sue Pearson collection
Photo: Sue Pearson

Maker unknown (possibly Dean's), circa 1960s

13 inches. Gold mohair, brown velvet feet. Plastic safety eyes. Stuffed with chipped foam. Non-working growler. Embroidered nose.

Value: Good $ 125
      Fair $ 100
      Poor $ 35

Donna McPherson collection
Photo: Donna McPherson

Left: Merrythought, Cheeky, circa 1960s

14 inches. Tan synthetic plush, amber plastic eyes, velveteen inset snout. Felt hand pads, brushed fabric foot pads and ear lining. Cloth tag on right foot.

Value:	Good	$ 350
	Fair	$ 250
	Poor	$ 100

Right: Forsum (Japan), circa 1969

10 inches. Apricot synthetic plush, velveteen pads and inset snout, amber glass eyes. Sliced-in ears. Cloth tush tag "1969. Forsum // made in Japan."

Value:	Good	$ 150
	Fair	$ 100
	Poor	$ 50

Don and Helene Marlowe collection
Photo: Don and Helene Marlowe

Maker unknown, circa 1960s

16 inches. White mohair. Black floss nose with traces of red floss tongue. Plastic "googly" eyes. Soft stuffing.

Value:	Good	$ 250
	Fair	$ 175
	Poor	$ 75

Michaud collection
Photo: T. Michaud

Left: Maker unknown, circa 1960s

14 inches. Cotton plush.

Value: Good $ 150
       Fair $ 100
       Poor $ 50

Center: Chad Valley, circa 1960s

16 inches. Fair condition.

Value: Good $ 300
       Fair $ 225
       Poor $ 100

Right: Maker unknown, circa 1960s

12 inches. Cotton plush.

Value: Good $ 150
       Fair $ 100
       Poor $ 50

Sue Pearson collection
Photo: Sue Pearson

Additional Listings, not pictured

Merrythought, pajama bag (night-dress case), circa 1960s

20 inches. Mohair with dark brown pads. Foot label on right foot pad.

Value: Good $ 350
       Fair $ 250
       Poor $ 100

Chad Valley, circa 1961

12 inches. Gold mohair. Glass eyes. Excelsior and kapok stuffing. Foot label reads "Chad Valley Co. Ltd. By appointment with Queen Elizabeth the Queen Mother."

Value: Good $ 400
       Fair $ 275
       Poor $ 100

Wendy Boston, circa 1964

16 inches. Light-gold synthetic plush. Unjointed. Plastic eyes. Foam chip stuffing. Maker's label sewn into side seam of bear.

Value: Good $ 200
       Fair $ 150
       Poor $ 50

Maker unknown (Holland), circa 1960s

12 inches. Unjointed. Mohair and rayon fabric. Excelsior and kapok stuffing. Unusual face.

Value: Good $ 150
Fair $ 100
Poor $ 50

Donna McPherson collection
Photo: Donna McPherson

Maker unknown (Japan), school set, circa 1960s

Teacher, 5 inches, students, 3½ inches. This is similar to a set made by Steiff. This set is of poor quality and was made for Shackman. Yellow rayon jointed bears. Glass eyes, plastic nose, no mouth.

Value: Good $ 200
Fair $ 150
Poor $ 75

Donna McPherson collection
Photo: Donna McPherson

1970-2000

Steiff, Baloo, circa 1980

11 inches. Felt claws on paws and feet.With chest tag and button w/paper label in ear. Store stock.

Value: Good $ 300
　　　　Fair $ 200
　　　　Poor $ 100

Michaud collection
Photo: T. Michaud

Steiff, store display, circa 1983

18 inches with stand. This is reported to be one of only ten pieces made for Hans Otto Steiff's U.S. tour in 1983. The bear is a replica of a 1909 Steiff bear and has a brass button in his ear.

Value: Good $ 1,000
　　　　Fair $ 700
　　　　Poor $ 300

Susan and Steve Swickard collection
Photo: T. Michaud

Steiff, bear on wheels, circa 1985

6¼ inches long, 5 inches high. This is a replica of an early Steiff bear on wheels.

Value: Good $ 250
　　　　Fair $ 175
　　　　Poor $ 75

Delores Buntz collection
Photo: Robert Buntz

Additional Listings, not pictured

Steiff, Petsy, circa 1970s

15 inches. Caramel dralon plush.

Value:			
Good	$	350
Fair	$	250
Poor	$	100

Steiff, mini panda, circa 1972

4½ inches. Black-and-white mohair. Bendable limbs. Mint in original box.

Value:			
Good	$	500
Fair	$	200
Poor	$	75

Steiff, Nimrod Teddy Roosevelt set, circa 1983

8½ inches. Limited edition of 10,000. In original box. Wears green felt hat, orange felt jacket, imitation leather boots.

Value:			
Good	$	475
Fair	$	300
Poor	$	100

Steiff, Mama & Baby, circa 1984

16 inches and 7¼ inches. Limited edition of 16,000. Giengen Birthplace set.

Value:			
Good	$	475
Fair	$	300
Poor	$	100

Steiff, Giengen Teddy Bear set, circa 1985

Two bears, 13 inches, and 4-inch baby in cradle.

Value:			
Good	$	300
Fair	$	200
Poor	$	100

Steiff, bears on a wigwag (teeter totter), circa 1988

9-inch gold bear and 7-inch chocolate-brown bear on a metal frame with wooden wheels. Limited to edition of 4,000. Boxed. Replica of 1909 original.

Value:			
Good	$	250
Fair	$	175
Poor	$	75

Steiff, circa 1984

16½ inches. Brown mohair with leather paw and foot pads. Original paper chest tag.

Value:			
Good	$	200
Fair	$	150
Poor	$	75

Steiff, Petsy pair, circa 1984

Each 11 inches. Boy in Lederhosen; Girl in Dirndl.

Value (pair):			
Good	$	500
Fair	$	350
Poor	$	150

Steiff, Margaret Strong bride and groom, 1984

14 and 14½ inches. Costumed pair.

Value (pair):			
Good	$	950
Fair	$	650
Poor	$	275

Steiff, Papa bear, circa 1980

17 inches. Limited edition of 11,000.

Value:			
Good	$	1,200
Fair	$	850
Poor	$	350

Steiff, polar bear, circa 1987

4½ inches. Limited edition of 3,000. Jointed legs and head. Replica of 1909 original.

Value: Good $ 650
      Fair $ 450
      Poor $ 200

Steiff, circa 1988

15½ inches. Black mohair with leather nose. Limited edition of 4,000.

Value: Good $ 900
      Fair $ 650
      Poor $ 200

Steiff, Goldilocks and The Three Bears set, circa 1984

Goldilocks is a 16-inch Suzanne Gibson doll; three bears are Papa, 13 inches, Mama, 12 inches, and Baby, 10 inches. Limited edition of 2,000 sets.

Value: Good $ 750
      Fair $ 400
      Poor $ 175

Steiff Teddy Tea Party set, circa 1982

Four bears, each 7 inches, with porcelain tea set. Limited edition of 10,000 sets.

Value: Good $ 600
      Fair $ 425
      Poor $ 175

Steiff, Jackie, circa 1986

10 inches. Limited edition of 10,000. Boxed. Replica of 1953 teddy.

Value: Good $ 300
      Fair $ 200
      Poor $ 100

Same bear, 13½ inches.

Value: Good $ 400
      Fair $ 275
      Poor $ 125

Steiff, Passport bear, circa 1985

15½ inches. Bear comes with his own passport.

Value: Good $ 275
      Fair $ 200
      Poor $ 75

Steiff, circa 1986

11 inches, Girl bear in sailor dress.

Value: Good $ 225
      Fair $ 150
      Poor $ 75

Steiff, musical Mr. Cinnamon, circa 1990

10½ inches. Exclusive edition for Harrod's department store, England. Limited edition of 2,000.

Value: Good $ 650
      Fair $ 450
      Poor $ 200

Steiff, Alfonzo, circa 1990

13½ inches. Red mohair with silk tunic. Produced exclusively for Teddy Bears of Witney, England. Limited edition of 5,000.

Value:	Good	$	950
	Fair	$	650
	Poor	$	275

Steiff, baby Alfonzo, circa 1995

9½ inches. Smaller version of 1990 edition. Produced exclusively for Teddy Bears of Witney, England. Limited edition of 5,000.

Value:	Good	$	350
	Fair	$	250
	Poor	$	100

Steiff, muzzle bear, circa 1990

13½ inches. White mohair replica of 1908 original. Limited edition of 6,000.

Value:	Good	$	325
	Fair	$	225
	Poor	$	100

Steiff, Otto, circa 1992

14 inches. USA exclusive. U.S. flag on foot pad. Limited edition of 5,000.

Value:	Good	$	500
	Fair	$	350
	Poor	$	150

Steiff, brown bear, circa 1993

25 inches. Replica of 1907 original. UK exclusive. Limited edition of 3,000.

Value:	Good	$	850
	Fair	$	600
	Poor	$	250

Steiff, Baloo, circa 1995

14 inches. Limited edition of 2,500 for Walt Disney World Teddy Bear & Doll Convention.

Value:	Good	$	500
	Fair	$	350
	Poor	$	150

Steiff, Reggie, circa 1997

15 inches. Wears Safari jacket and hat, campaign buttons and African Diary book. Boxed.

Value:	Good	$	375
	Fair	$	250
	Poor	$	100

Steiff, circa 1997

12 inches. Commemorates Steiff founder's 150th birthday. Bear wears a ceramic disc with Margarete Steiff's photo on it.

Value:	Good	$	200
	Fair	$	150
	Poor	$	75

Steiff, Giengen Festival bear, circa 1997

12 inches. Blackey.

Value:	Good	$	700
	Fair	$	500
	Poor	$	200

Steiff, Giengen Festival bear, circa 1998

12 inches. Whitey.

Value:	Good	$	600
	Fair	$	425
	Poor	$	175

Steiff, Giengen Festival bear, circa 1999

12 inches. Rosey.

Value:	Good	$	600
	Fair	$	425
	Poor	$	175

Hermann, no-no bear, circa 1985

4½ inches. Black mohair.

Value:	Good	$	150
	Fair	$	100
	Poor	$	50

Hermann Spielwaren GmbH Adelheid, circa 1991

11 inches. Blond mohair. Green ribbon on neck. Green triangle plastic trademark on chest. With certificate. Limited edition of 200.

Value:	Good	$	175
	Fair	$	125
	Poor	$	50

Teddy Hermann, Teddy workshop, circa 1993

24½ inches. Red seal reads "Hermann Teddy Original." Limited edition of 1,000.

Value:	Good	$	750
	Fair	$	525
	Poor	$	225

Teddy Hermann, Nostalgic Ted, circa 1994

12 inches. Old gold mohair.

Value:	Good	$	100
	Fair	$	75
	Poor	$	25

Same bear, 16 inches

Value:	Good	$	150
	Fair	$	100
	Poor	$	50

Same bear, 20 inches

Value:	Good	$	200
	Fair	$	150
	Poor	$	60

Teddy Hermann, Strawberry bear, circa 1998

16 inches. Limited edition of 800.

Value:	Good	$	200
	Fair	$	150
	Poor	$	60

Clemens, Flickenbar, circa 1995

14 inches. Limited edition of 250.

Value:	Good	$	150
	Fair	$	100
	Poor	$	40

Clemens, miniature, circa 1995

6 inches. Named Mustard.

Value:	Good	$	75
	Fair	$	50
	Poor	$	25

Grisly Spielwaren, Classic Teddy, circa 1997

4½ inches. Honey mohair.

Value:	Good	$	50
	Fair	$	35
	Poor	$	15

Grisly Spielwaren, circa 1998

14 inches. Named Julia. Limited edition of 888.

Value:	Good	$	125
	Fair	$	85
	Poor	$	35

Grisly Spielwaren, circa 1998

14 inches. Named Leonie. Limited edition of 179.

Value:	Good	$	150
	Fair	$	100
	Poor	$	50

House of Nisbet (England), circa 1977

12 inches. Modacrylic plush fabric. Jointed. Plastic safety eyes. Made to celebrate the Queen's Jubilee.

Value: Good $ 150
Fair $ 100
Poor $ 50

Michaud collection
Photo: T. Michaud

Andy Panda (United States), circa 1982

Licensed by Walter Lantz Production Inc. Bear is shown with a 16mm film and box of the popular cartoon character of the same name.

Value: Good $ 100
Fair $ 70
Poor $ 30

Susan and Steve Swickard collection
Photo: T. Michaud

Annalee (United States), Santa, circa 1988

9 inches. A highly collectible line by an American firm with a large following in both the doll and teddy world. Felt dolls and animals are their mainstay. Airbrushed highlights. Santa's bag is burlap. Felt sun is a special pin that did not come with Santa.

Value: Good $ 250
Fair $ 175
Poor $ 75

Michaud collection
Photo: T. Michaud

Additional Listings, not pictured

Merrythought (England), Cheeky, circa 1970s

17 inches. Light gray plush with felt pads. Label on right foot pad.

Value: Good $ 250
       Fair $ 170
       Poor $ 75

Merrythought (England), circa 1970s

17 inches. Wool and synthetic blend. Labeled.

Value: Good $ 150
       Fair $ 100
       Poor $ 50

Merrythought (England), Guardsman, circa 1970s

21 inches. Mohair head, paws and feet. Guardsman uniform part of body. Bear wears traditional busby.

Value: Good $ 200
       Fair $ 150
       Poor $ 60

Pedigree (England), circa 1970s

16 inches. Rust-colored synthetic plush, plastic eyes and nose.

Value: Good $ 100
       Fair $ 70
       Poor $ 30

Maker unknown (England), Rupert, circa 1970s

14 inches. White plush with traditional yellow checked pants and scarf, red jumper (clothing is part of body).

Value: Good $ 50
       Fair $ 30
       Poor $ 10

Merrythought (England), circa 1980s

15 inches. Label on right foot pad. Medium-nap, pale-gold mohair. Felt pads.

Value: Good $ 150
       Fair $ 100
       Poor $ 50

Dakin (United States), koala, circa 1979

13 inches. Short beige plush with off-white belly. Brown plastic eyes and nose. Sewn-in label and hang tag.

Value: Good $ 50
       Fair $ 30
       Poor $ 10

Dakin, (United States), Misha, circa 1979

12 inches. Produced for Olympics held in Russia, from which the United States withdrew—which makes the symbol bear even more collectible. Brown and tan short plush, plastic eyes and nose. Wears belt and buckle with Olympic symbol.

Value: Good $ 150
       Fair $ 100
       Poor $ 35

Raikes by Applause (United States), Eric, circa 1985

14 inches. Wears ski sweater, scarf and cap.

Value: Good $ 600
       Fair $ 425
       Poor $ 175

Raikes by Applause (United States), Bentley, circa 1985

16 inches. Wears tweed vest.
Box and certificate.

Value: Good $ 350
       Fair $ 250
       Poor $ 100

Raikes by Applause (United States), Tyrone, circa 1986

36 inches. Medium-brown plush.
Wears black tuxedo with white shirt.

Value: Good $ 750
       Fair $ 525
       Poor $ 225

Raikes by Applause (United States), Penelope,circa 1986

16 inches. Wears pink party dress.
Box and certificate.

Value: Good $ 550
       Fair $ 375
       Poor $ 175

Raikes by Applause (United States), Cecil, circa 1986

16 inches. Limited edition of 15,000.
Glamour Bears of the 20's series. Dressed
as movie director in khaki Safari jacket,
satin ascot, red beret. Wears a monocle
and holds a megaphone.

Value: Good $ 250
       Fair $ 175
       Poor $ 75

Raikes by Applause (United States), Maude, circa 1986

20 inches. Limited edition of 15,000.
Glamour Bears of the 20's series.
Off-white fur. Wears flapper dress
and long string of pearls, pink felt hat.

Value: Good $ 300
       Fair $ 225
       Poor $ 100

Raikes by Applause (United States), Lindy, circa 1986

20 inches. Limited edition of 15,000.
Glamour Bears of the 20's series.
Medium-brown fur. Wears brown flight
jacket, pilot's cap, goggles and white
scarf.

Value: Good $ 500
       Fair $ 350
       Poor $ 150

Raikes by Applause (United States), Nurse, circa 1987

16 inches. Limited edition of 7,500.
Americana collection. Wears traditonal
nurse's uniform. Boxed. Hard to find.

Value: Good $ 300
       Fair $ 200
       Poor $ 100

Raikes by Applause (United States), Sweet Sunday collection, circa 1988

Three pieces: Sally, Susie and Timmy.
Each 15 inches. Dressed.
In original box.

Value (set):   Good $ 550
                Fair $ 375
                Poor $ 175

Raikes by Applause (United States), Mr. & Mrs Clause, circa 1988

17 inches high. White fur bears in
holiday outfits of velveteen. Boxed,
with certificate.

Value (pair):   Good $ 400
                 Fair $ 275
                 Poor $ 125

Raikes by Applause (United States), Andrew, circa 1988

14 inches. Limited edition of 5,000. Light-brown fur, wears shirt, tie and jacket. Hang tag and original box.

Value:	Good	$	175
	Fair	$	125
	Poor	$	50

Dayton Hudson department-store Santa, (United States), circa 1986

17 inches. White plush bear. Wears knitted red-and-green stocking cap (dated) and scarf.

Value:	Good	$	50
	Fair	$	35
	Poor	$	15

❖Christmas bears were a hot promotional item in many stores during the 1980s, and this tradition continues today. The bears were mass-produced overseas, generally in open editions. Because so many were marketed, few of them retain much value on the secondary market today.

Gund (United States), Collectors' Classic, circa 1983

12 inches. Jointed bear in gray plush. Boxed.

Value:	Good	$	50
	Fair	$	35
	Poor	$	15

Gund (United States), Gundy, circa 1985

8 inches. White plush. Hang tags and box.

Value:	Good	$	40
	Fair	$	25
	Poor	$	10

Gund (United States), Christmas bear, circa 1987

Light brown plush. Sold exclusively at J.C. Penney stores. Tag reads "Bear with No Name." Original price was $40.

Value:	Good	$	75
	Fair	$	50
	Poor	$	25

Gund (United States,) 90th year commemorative bear, circa 1988

16 inches. Tan plush. Red leather tag on chest.

Value:	Good	$	100
	Fair	$	75
	Poor	$	25

Gund (United States), Collectors' Classic, circa 1989

9½ inches. Light-brown plush, velveteen paw pads. Jointed. Chest tag, original box.

Value:	Good	$	50
	Fair	$	25
	Poor	$	10

Dean's Company (England), The Professor, circa 1995

19 inches. Michaud design. Black knit sweater, glasses.

Value:		
Good	$	250
Fair	$	175
Poor	$	75

Dean's Company (England), Grandpa Terry, circa 1996

9 inches. Michaud design. Limited edition of 2,000.

Value:		
Good	$	100
Fair	$	70
Poor	$	30

Dean's Company (England), Grandma Doris, circa 1997

8 inches. Michaud design. Limited edition of 1,000.

Value:		
Good	$	100
Fair	$	70
Poor	$	30

Dean's Company (England), circa 1995

21 inches. Named Clarence. Limited edition of 1,000.

Value:		
Good	$	150
Fair	$	100
Poor	$	50

Dean's Company (England), circa 1996

18 inches. Mohair. Re-creation of 1937 green bear. Limited edition of 250.

Value:		
Good	$	200
Fair	$	150
Poor	$	50

Dean's Company (England), Mycroft bear, circa 1995

16 inches. Limited edition of 500.

Value:		
Good	$	200
Fair	$	150
Poor	$	50

Dean's Company (England) Red, white, blue bear, circa 1996

7 inches. Mohair. Limited edition of 1,000.

Value:		
Good	$	100
Fair	$	70
Poor	$	30

Dean's Company (England), circa 1994

15 inches. Named Russel. Limited edition of 1,500.

Value:		
Good	$	175
Fair	$	125
Poor	$	50

Canterbury (England), circa 1993

32 inches. Flash, the company mascot bear. Long rust-colored plush with authentic campaign medals and glasses.

Value:		
Good	$	600
Fair	$	425
Poor	$	175

Merrythought (England), Cheeky, circa 1997

8 inches. Re-issue. Limited edition of 1,000.

Value:		
Good	$	200
Fair	$	150
Poor	$	60

Raikes by Applause
(United States), circa 1991

15 inches. 4th Christmas Edition.
Nicolette. Dark brown plush.
Girl bear wears red cotton print
dress and bonnet. Holds a Christmas
stocking. Traditional Raikes
wood face.

Value:	Good	$	200
	Fair	$	150
	Poor	$	60

R. John Wright
(United States), Wintertime
Pooh & Piglet, circa 1994

Pooh: 5 inches. Mohair plush, fully jointed. Piglet: 2½ inches. Felt, jointed neck
and arms. Froduced exclusively for
F.A.O. Schwarz. Limited edition of 250
pairs.

Value (pair):	Good	$	1,500
	Fair	$	1,000
	Poor	$	450

The following listings are for Muffy Vanderbear, produced by the North American Bear Company (United States). Dates indicate year of introduction. All pieces are retired.

Muffy Pilgrim, circa 1989

Wears black dress with full lace-trimmed skirt, black belt with silver buckle, white collar and white pilgrim hat.

Value:	Good	$	40
	Fair	$	30
	Poor	$	10

Muffy Little Fir Tree, circa 1990

Boxed limited edition. Wears organdy and satin green dress with a headdress trimmed in holly and stars. Green satin slippers.

Value:	Good	$	250
	Fair	$	175
	Poor	$	75

Muffy Ginger Bear, circa 1992

Boxed limited edition. Wears cookie outfit in brown velour with white icing and gumdrop buttons. Box is in gingerbread house design.

Value:	Good	$	75
	Fair	$	50
	Poor	$	20

Muffy Snowflake, circa 1993

Boxed limited edition.Wears silver-colored snowflake costume with jacket and velvet skirt, snowflake crown and iridescent wand.

Value:	Good	$	40
	Fair	$	25
	Poor	$	10

Muffy 10th Anniversary, circa 1994

Boxed limited edition. Wears lavender taffeta gown hemmed in gold braid. The scalloped overskirt is trimmed with pansies and painted gold leaves and ribbons. She also wears a crown with ten candles on it.

Value:	Good	$	80
	Fair	$	55
	Poor	$	20

Additional Listings, not pictured

The Littlest Cowpoke from The Wild West: A Traveling Rodeo Show collection, circa 1991

Wears red-and-white checked dress, red bandana-printed pinafore, blue felt cowboy hat.

Value:			
	Good	$	60
	Fair	$	40
	Poor	$	15

Down on the Farm, circa 1992

Wears blue-and-white checked sun dress, kerchief and blue shoes. Carries a sack of "Muffy's Farm Feed."

Value:			
	Good	$	60
	Fair	$	40
	Poor	$	15

A Highland Fling from The Scottish Collection, circa 1993

Wears Scottish outfit with plaid kilt, red sweater, tam with yellow pom-pom and a sporan (type of Scottish purse) on her waist.

Value:			
	Good	$	45
	Fair	$	30
	Poor	$	10

Muffy of the North, circa 1994

Boxed limited edition. Wears white Eskimo outfit with hood. Comes with a white seal.

Value:			
	Good	$	50
	Fair	$	35
	Poor	$	15

New England Country Christmas, circa 1995

Wears lace-trimmed green gingham dress, muslin pinafore, white felt boots, and comes with a calico kitten.

Value:			
	Good	$	50
	Fair	$	35
	Poor	$	15

Take a Hike from A Walk on the Wylde Side collection, circa 1996

Muffy and Hoppy (rabbit) set: Muffy wears feather-print jacket, plaid shorts and hat. Hoppy wears gold-thistle print jacket, plaid shorts and hiking hat.

Value (pair) :			
	Good	$	80
	Fair	$	55
	Poor	$	25

Little Peddlar Twelve Days of Christmas set, circa 1997

Wears goose shoes and hat with a partridge in a pear tree embroidered on it. Carries a basket of geese. Limited edition of 5,000 designed for the 10th anniversary Walt Disney World Teddy Bear and Doll convention.

Value:			
	Good	$	200
	Fair	$	150
	Poor	$	60

Muffy Little Bear Peep, circa 1998

Numbered and boxed limited edition of 15,000. Wears a bright yellow and lavender outfit and comes with her own Mary the Lamb.

Value:			
	Good	$	60
	Fair	$	40
	Poor	$	15

Muffy Candy C'angel, circa 1997

Boxed limited edition. Wears candy-cane-striped dress, wings in a candy-cane theme and candy-cane halo above her head.

Value:			
	Good	$	40
	Fair	$	25
	Poor	$	10

Muffy Sugar Plum Fairy, circa 1998

Boxed limited edition. Wears sugar-plum outfit with iridescent wings and carries a basket filled with sugar plums.

Value:			
	Good	$	45
	Fair	$	30
	Poor	$	10

All of the following bears are produced by the Boyds company (United States). All are fully jointed.

Clement, circa 1990

16 inches. Russet color, light-tan paw pads. Unclothed. Retired 1992.

Value:			
Good	$	150
Fair	$	100
Poor	$	40

Otto Von Bruin, circa 1992

6 inches. Gold plush with beige paw pads. This bear was a Golden Teddy Award winner. Retired 1994.

Value:			
Good	$	48
Fair	$	32
Poor	$	15

Auntie Alice, circa 1993

10 inches. Wears black hat with roses on it and purple ribbon on neck. Retired 1996.

Value:			
Good	$	40
Fair	$	25
Poor	$	10

Homer, circa 1993

8 inches. Wears a baseball uniform and carries his own bat. Retired 1996.

Value:			
Good	$	45
Fair	$	30
Poor	$	10

Bailey, circa 1994

8 inches. Wears a blue checkered dress with lace collar, red cape. Retired 1995.

Value:			
Good	$	58
Fair	$	40
Poor	$	15

Rupert, 1994

8 inches. White plush with red sweater that features a snowflake design on front. Retired 1996.

Value:			
Good	$	48
Fair	$	30
Poor	$	10

Chan, 1994

6 inches. Wears white bunny suit. Retired 1998.

Value:			
Good	$	30
Fair	$	20
Poor	$	8

Roosevelt, circa 1995

8 inches. Wears knit sweater in red, white and blue. Retired 1996.

Value:			
Good	$	45
Fair	$	30
Poor	$	10

Edmund, circa 1995

8 inches. Wears knit sweater with Christmas tree design on front. Retired 1996.

Value:			
Good	$	48
Fair	$	30
Poor	$	10

Emma, circa 1995

14 inches. Wears blue-checkered dress with red checkered hearts on it and blue-checkered bow in hair. Retired 1997.

Value:			
Good	$	45
Fair	$	30
Poor	$	10

Philomena, circa 1995

14 inches. Golden-brown plush. Wears blue-plaid dress covering tan pantaloons and tan bib, with blue-plaid ribbon on head.

Value:			
Good	$	50
Fair	$	35
Poor	$	10

Bailey and Mathew, circa 1996

Each 8 inches. The set comes with resin ornaments in their image. Bailey wears a light-colored sweater with houses on it and a denim skirt and hat. Mathew wears a light-colored sweater and denim pants. Retired 1996.

Value (pair with figurines): Good $100
Fair $ 70
Poor $ 30

Rex, circa 1996

8 inches. Tan plush. Wears knitted romper suit. Retired 1998.

Value: Good $ 50
Fair $ 35
Poor $ 15

Burl, circa 1996

10 inches. Golden-brown plush. Wears plaid overalls. Retired 1998.

Value: Good $ 40
Fair $ 25
Poor $ 10

Cornwallis, circa 1996

16 inches. Dark-brown plush. Wears knit off-white sweater with front panel design featuring a red heart. Retired 1997.

Value: Good $ 75
Fair $ 50
Poor $ 20

Edmund, circa 1996

8 inches. Wears knit sweater and gray pants. Retired 1997.

Value: Good $ 45
Fair $ 30
Poor $ 10

Evelyn, circa 1997

10 inches. Light-brown plush. Wears red-plaid dress, velveteen bloomers and hat. Retired 1998.

Value: Good $ 45
Fair $ 30
Poor $ 10

Hans Q. Berryman, circa 1997

6 inches. Winter-white plush. Wears blue-knit sweater.

Value:			
	Good	$	45
	Fair	$	30
	Poor	$	10

Augusta, circa 1998

14 inches. Wears denim dress and straw hat with flower. Hard to find. Retired 1998.

Value:			
	Good	$	60
	Fair	$	40
	Poor	$	15

Ethan, circa 1998

9 inches. White plush. Wears patariotic red, white and blue sweater. Retired 1999.

Value:			
	Good	$	50
	Fair	$	35
	Poor	$	10

Sandy Claus II, circa 1998

16 inches. All plush, including Santa outfit which is part of body, arms & legs. Jointed.

Value:			
	Good	$	35
	Fair	$	20
	Poor	$	10

Fillmore, circa 1998

16 inches. Golden-tan mohair with shaved muzzle and suede leather pads. Wears black-and-tan houndstooth pants and a red-and-gray checked sweater with brass buttons. Also carries a small airplane. Made exlusively for QVC. Retired 1999.

Value:			
	Good	$	100
	Fair	$	70
	Poor	$	30

Boyds classic Pooh "A Christmas to Remember," circa 1999

15 inches. Gold mohair. Fully jointed. Wears the traditional red sweater with "Pooh" embroidered in gold.

Value (with box):			
	Good	$	150
	Fair	$	100
	Poor	$	40

❖ Boyds mohair bears carry a stronger value on the secondary market than the plush bears, due to the higher quality of the material.

The Market for Contemporary Artist-Made Teddy Bears

The artist-made teddy bear is a relatively new phenomenon; it began in the mid-to-late 1970s and established itself strongly over the following decade. (Our definition of a teddy bear artist is one who creates his or her own designs, and crafts the bear in whole, or in part, by him- or herself.) It would be safe to say there are literally thousands of teddy bear artists in today's market, not even counting the large number of skilled bear makers who work from someone else's pattern.

These skilled artists perform a significant role in the bear world. In fact, many manufacturers regularly contract with artists to produce designs for manufacture. It is initially surprising, then, to realize that only a small percentage of artist-made teddy bears have been offered on the secondary market. In fact, a secondary market for these pieces is relatively non-existent. The primary reason for this lack of a secondary market is that most of these bears are still being enjoyed by the original collectors who are not ready to give them up. What's more, most artists produce a relatively small number of teddy bears each year; many of them create primarily one-of-a-kinds or very small editions of five to ten pieces. All this leaves the secondary market rather barren of the artists' work, and certainly does not provide enough information to establish a fair-market value.

We wanted to offer some reasonable values for contemporary artist-made bears, so after much reflection and discussion with others in this field, we determined upon the following solution. We selected a number of artists who have been creating and selling teddy bears for more than a decade. We asked for an example of a basic design they have produced for a number of years and still offer today, the piece's original price at issue, and the price it sells for today. This information demonstrates how a particular artist's work has grown in value. While some of the cost is due to yearly inflation, for the most part, the increase reflects the growing popularity of the artist.

We believe that the following examination of prices for artist bears demonstrates a fair-market value for the work featured. If you strike an average increase for the bears listed, you can apply that increase to the work of an artist who has had the equivalent experience in order to determine a fair price for his or her work. The final determining factor, as always, is the agreement between buyer and seller that will set the market value for a given piece.

THE BEAR LADY

Monty & Joe Sours
2418 Redbud Road
Golden City, MO 64748
Phone/fax: (417) 535-8340
Web page:
www.teddybears.com/art/sours

This internationally known couple made their first bear in 1981 and have been supplying collectors here and abroad since that time. They have won numerous awards for their work and are among the few artists who have actually produced a bear from scratch; that is, they raised the goats, sheared them, spun the mohair, crafted the fabric, designed and created the bear! They have done the same with alpaca.

Top Left: Gnarley was created in 1987. He is 21 inches high, mohair with wool pads, glass eyes. Polyester and pellet stuffing.
　　Original price (1987): $ 139.95
　　Current price　　　　 $ 219.95

Top Right: Gnarley Jr., 15 inches high, was introduced in 1988 and has the same features as his big brother.
　　Original price (1988) $ 99.95
　　Current price　　　　 $ 159.95

Center: Wilbur was introduced in 1988. This 11-inch free-standing bear is mohair with wool pads, glass eyes and polyester stuffing. He wears a felt beanie with hand-carved propeller.
　　Original price (1988) $ 109.95
　　Current price　　　　 $ 179.95

Bottom: Anastasia was first produced in 1989. She is a 15-inch free-standing mohair bear with wool pads, glass eyes and polyester stuffing.
　　Original price (1989) $ 179.95
　　Current price　　　　 $ 249.95

CHINA CUPBOARD
Cindy McGuire
519 S. Main Street
Marion, OH 43302
(740) 387-7742

Cindy McGuire first employed her design and sewing skills in the doll world, and soon branched out into teddy bears. This artist has traveled extensively to shows here and abroad and works primarily in mohair. Her business has grown from its humble beginnings into a cottage industry.

Pearl Rose was first created in 1994 and continues to be one of Cindy's best sellers today. The pale-pink mohair bear has polyfil stuffing, wool felt pads and glass eyes. The clothing is hand crafted by the artist. There have been subtle changes to the pattern, but the basic design remains the same.

Original price (1994): $ 150
Current price $ 220

CM BEARS
Carol Martin
53 N. Main Street
Eureka Springs, AR 72632
(501) 253-0695

Carol Martin crafted her first teddy in 1984. She and her husband Henry are retired teachers who also run a teddy bear store. Carol produces most of her designs in mohair, and her teddies are noted for their center-seam heads, brass name tags and above-average weight.

One of Carol's very first designs, which she continues to craft today, is Bare Bear, a limited edition of 500, which has recently reached the 380 mark.

Original price (1987) $ 59
Current price $ 100

H.L. Bear is a 12-inch mohair bear that Carol has produced since 1989. It has been crafted in a variety of colors and types of mohair, including the one shown in a beautiful deep-pile rust color mohair.

Original price	$	62
Current price	$	100

HAPPY TYMES COLLECTIBLES

Bev White
399 Echo Dell Road
Downingtown, PA 19335
(610) 873-0407
FAX 610-873- 5163
Email: happytymes@chesco.com

Bev White is another artist who turned from dolls to teddy bears; she created her first bear in 1985. Collectors have come to expect the unique and unusual from this artist, and they are never disappointed. In addition to crafting bears that she sells at shows throughout the world, Bev designs for three manufacturers and started her own line of manufactured teddies in 1997.

Above: An all-time favorite with collectors is Bev's Mr. Brewster Button Bear, a 20-inch-high signature piece.

Original price (1990)	$225
Current price	$400

Right: Bev created a mohair limited-edition Stan and Ollie Portrait set in 1993 that sold for $995. The edition of 75 sold out quickly, but a set sold on the secondary market in 1999 for $1,800.

HUG-A-BEAR

Janet Reeves
640 E. Wheeler Rd.
Midland, MI 48640
Phone/fax: 517-631-3625

Michigan teddy artist Janet Reeves has been designing and crafting bears since the early 1980s. Some of her creations are inspired by the fabrics she works with, primarily mohair and alpaca. Janet's line includes one-of-a-kinds, limited editions and special orders. She is a regular on the show circuit, attending more than 15 shows a year.

Top: Amanda is a 12-inch caramel mohair bear first produced by Janet in 1986 as a limited edition of 275. It won the Golden Teddy award in 1987.

Original price (1986)	$	110
Current price	$	190

Center: Lucy Locket, 13 inches high, was Janet's first bear in her Nursery Rhyme series. It was first crafted in 1989.

Original price (1989)	$	190
Current price	$	270

Bottom: Otis is 11½ inches tall and crafted of string mohair. He is a free-standing bear first produced by Janet in 1991.

Original price (1991)	$	130
Current price	$	185

Eileen Rosolowski-Kaiser

1181 E. Cottage Grove Rd.
Linwood, MI 48684
(517) 697-3875

Eileen is another artist who crossed over from the world of doll making to teddy bear making. Her first teddy design was crafted in 1985, and she has since developed a strong following for her work. Eileen specializes in one-of-a-kind dressed bears and also does open edition "bare" bears. Her daughter Marjorie Engelhardt now creates miniature bears, which gives the two many happy hours working together. Eileen had long resisted naming her bears, leaving that to her customers, but she has recently started to market them with names.

Top: The Red-white-blue bear is one of Eileen's basic designs, first crafted in 1990. She has since created several interesting spin-offs of this design, working with various fabrics, including some hand-dyed mohair.

Original price (1990)	$	65
Current price	$	122

Right: This multicolored bear of hand-dyed mohair is a variation of Eileen's original pattern. This model currently sells for $160.

MILL CREEK CREATIONS

Rosalie Frischmann
6793 Baker Rd.
Arena, WI 53503
(608) 753-2327
FAX 608-753-2017
Email: milcreek@mhtc.net

This Wisconsin artist is well known throughout the world not only for her teddies with sweet expressions, but also for her animal creations, particularly her puppies, and she frequently creates teddies that come with their own puppy. Rosalie created her first bear in 1983 and exhibits at shows here and abroad. She also creates designs for Gund.

One of Frischmann's first efforts was 11-inch "Little Gert," which sold in 1986 for $95. She has expanded on that pattern and done several variations, including her 11-inch sweater bears with glass eyes, ultra-suede paw pads and hand-embroidered features.

Original price (1986)	$	95
Current price	$	250

NOSTALGIC BEARS

Sue & Randall Foskey
Rt. 1 Box 68
Ocean View, DE 19970
800-289-8339
FAX 302-539-8965
Email: nostalgicbears@dol.net

Sue and Randall Foskey work full time producing and marketing their teddy bears. Sue was not happy with her very first effort at creating a teddy in 1982, so she spent a good deal of time studying antique bears and created her own patterns based upon the antique look. It was the beginning of a full time career for the couple, who now travel far and wide meeting collectors and attending shows and conventions.

Suzi and Bobbi are 8-inch no-no bears introduced by the Foskeys in 1986 in a limited edition of 100, which sold out. Moving the tail makes the head move. The bear was re-issued in 2000.

Original price (1986)	$	42
Current price	$	96

Money bear purse. Introduced in 1987 in plush. No longer available in this fabric. To show how an original concept can grow, the Foskeys' new design is avialable in mohair in a variety of colors. When the purse is opened, a growler in the head forewarns the owner!

Original price (plush-1987)	$	45
Current price (mohair)	$	180

The Black Bear introduced by the Foskeys in 1989 is the first in a series of six bears made in a limited edition of 100 each. The third edition won a Golden Teddy award in 1991. The bears are crafted in black and gold mohair with gold felt paw pads that have been silk-screened in black. Each series had different contrasting face and paw pad colors. All have leather collars and silk-screened paw pads.

Original price (1989)	$	90
Current price	$	175

In 1987 Sue and Randall issued their first antique-reproduction teddies. They were originally done in hand-distressed mohair, with excelsior stuffing and distressed felt paw pads. The trim was created from antique fabrics.

Original price, 9 inches (1987)	$	65
Current price	$	150
Original price, 17 inches (1987)	$	175
Current price	$	235

(Not shown is a 12-inch version that originally sold for $95 and now costs $175.)

Reference & Resources

Buying Antique Teddy Bears

One can occasionally find a charming vintage teddy in an antique shop, and a fair number of bears in our own collection have come from just such a source. With the advent of antique malls, you can literally shop at several hundred dealers with just one stop, and most of our traveling allows for that opportunity. You should note, however, that dealers who sell a wide range of antiques are rarely experts when it comes to teddy bears, so the information and price they offer may not be accurate or realistic. Most serious teddy bear collectors build a library of good books on the subject, and educate themselves on teddy bears, particularly the type they are attracted to.

There are a number of specialists who deal primarily or exclusively in vintage teddy bears, and these are usually your best source for buying bears. Specialists generally make it their business to be well-informed about what they are selling, and most of them stand behind their sale with a return privilege. They also typically have a much larger selection than you are likely to find even in the larger antique malls.

Probably the fastest-growing source for antique and collectible teddies is the internet, which has both pros and cons. On the plus side, it presents collectors with sources all around the world. On the down side, it, too, has attracted people who misrepresent what they are selling. They offer glowing descriptions of the bear and show one or more pictures, but there are things that cannot be seen in a photo. The biggest flaw that can render an old bear nearly worthless is dry rot, which may be a condition the seller is not even aware of. Sellers on auction sites rarely offer return privileges. Another major complaint from collectors who have made a purchase from an internet auction is the bear was saturated with a smoky, musty smell. While this situation has several remedies, you do not want to discover such a problem after paying a lot of money for your bear.

As a rule of thumb, the more you invest in a purchase, the more effort you should put into making sure you are getting what you are paying for.

Fakes and Copies

Identification of older bears can be difficult, even for the experienced dealer. It is not unusual to find mislabeled teddies offered for sale, either by error or, in some cases, deliberately. You can get an idea of just how widespread this practice is by viewing some of the listings for antique and vintage bears on the internet auction sites. Due to the strong demand for Steiff bears, many of the teddies listed are implied to be Steiff. In some instances they are flatly identified as such, but more often the listing will say "Steiff?" or "appears to be Steiff" or one of a score of suggestions to the viewer that this is a Steiff bear. As always, the rule is: "buyer beware ."

My favorite mis-identifaction story regards an individual who attempted to defraud a friend of ours by selling her a bear by mail that was purported to be an antique Steiff, complete with button. Once she received it, she turned it over to someone who regularly cleaned her bears, who promptly telephoned her. "There's something strange about this bear," she was told. "He has two buttons."

On closer examination, she discovered it not only had a Steiff button in the ear (placed there by the seller) but also had a small button under one arm. The bear turned out to be an excellent early example of a Bing bear, and it had more value than the "Steiff" the seller claimed it was! Now that's poetic justice.

As the value of old teddy bears has escalated, the business has attracted people who would not hesitate to cheat a buyer with a fraudulent teddy bear. We have been at general auctions where an unsuspecting collector has paid a large sum for a teddy that was not what it was represented to be. Once you have made such a purchase, there is generally little recourse for recovering your money unless you can prove there was an intent to defraud you. In many cases, the auctioneer is not aware the item is a fake, and has been taken in by the seller. Spotting a fake is not always easy, but there are some things you can look for to help you avoid a costly error.

- Smell the bear. If it is 75 years old, it will retain a certain "dusty" smell that is similar to the smell that hits you when you walk into an old attic. Typically, forgeries have no odor whatsoever.
- Does the fabric appear to be worn naturally, or does it have "clumps" of mohair that may have been intentionally pulled out?
- Check the area between the joints to see if the color of the mohair there is somewhat stronger than that on the body of the bear. Mohair on an old bear fades over time. Forgeries that have been recently put together (even those made from old fabric) will not show any differentiation in the color between the joints and the body.
- Check for materials that may not be appropriate for an older bear. For example, we have seen forgeries that used worn glove leather for paw and foot pads. In most cases, however, the bear a forgerer is trying to copy would have had felt pads, not leather.
- Check to see if the fabric may have been recently dyed by rubbing

your hand over the surface. We saw some rather poor fakes from Great Britain, which were made of old fabric, but dyed after the bear was constructed. The result was that the dye did not penetrate between the joints well, and the color between the joints was actually lighter than the outside of the bear!

Unfortunately, some of the makers producing fakes are getting better and better. (They could use their talent to make new bears and probably earn a better living!) The bottom line is, buyer beware! Always ask if the dealer offers a return privilege.

Selling Antique Teddy Bears

We are frequently asked: "how do I sell an old bear (or a collection)?" Often this is asked by someone who has inherited a bear or a collection, and has no knowledge of teddy bears. When someone brings an old bear to us that may have belonged to a family member, we always ask first if there isn't someone in the family that would like it as an heirloom. If not, we can steer the seller in several directions.

The first thing to do in order to determine the best course of action is to determine the fair market value for the bear. In other words, have it appraised. Once an appraisal has been made, the best way to get close to full value for a bear is to sell it directly to a collector. This usually means placing ads in teddy bear magazines or antiques journals. The ad should describe what is for sale and payment terms. Typically a seller will accept a money order and ship the bear immediately, or accept a check, and send the bear once the check clears the bank. This protects the seller.

The internet is also a means of selling bears. The cost is low, and there is the potential to reach many collectors throughout the world. When selling on the internet, it is even more important to protect yourself by asking for payment by money order (including cost of shipping and insurance), or waiting until a check clears before shipping.

In some cases, an owner does not want to take the time or trouble to advertise the bear, but wants to make a quick sale. The fastest way to do this is by selling to a dealer, who will pay you outright for the bear. A dealer will never pay as much for a teddy bear as a collector, however, because the dealer, who has spent a lot of time and money developing a following of collectors, must make a profit. Dealer markups vary, but as a rule of thumb, the more valuable the bear, the smaller a margin the dealer will take. As in buying a teddy bear, the best recourse is usually to sell to a dealer who specializes in teddy bears. Take several good photos of the bear, and send copies to several dealers, asking for their offer.

It is always good practice to include a SASE (self-addressed stamped envelope) when writing to a dealer in order to speed up the response.

Appraisals

Selling an entire collection can be accomplished in much the same way as we have outlined for a single teddy bear, but here it is even more important to get a professional appraisal so you know exactly what you have and can then determine your best course of action. An appraisal should be based upon a study of the bear "in person," not just on a photograph. It is not necessarily a good plan to go to the appraiser that charges the least. Let's look at two hypothetical examples.

Appraiser #1 only charges a few dollars. He examines the bear for a minute or so, then says that it's a bear all right, and could be quite old (gives no year). "Kindofa funny color. It's got some bad damage on the feet where somebody must have used ink on it or something. I could probably sell it for $200 and if you want to sell it, I'll pay you right now."

Appraiser #2 tells you in advance the cost of the appraisal (perhaps $25). This appraiser seems to take forever, carefully examining every minute detail of the bear, turning him over, examining every detail with a magnifying glass, etc. Finally, the appraiser says: "You've got a real treasure here. It's a Steiff teddy from the 1910 to 1915 era. He doesn't have the Steiff trademark button in his ear, but that's not unusual, as many of them were removed by concerned parents. That really does not effect his value that much. He is also an unusual color, as Steiff did not make that many in this beautiful rust-colored mohair. His foot pads do have a few small moth holes and you can see the dark color felt that Steiff used under the padding (not ink damage after all!). He shows a few wear spots where the mohair has some slight wear, but overall I would rate this teddy to be in very good, even exceptional, condition. You will also be pleased to know that your bear is valued in the range of $10,000 to $15,000." This appraiser may or may not be interested in buying the bear, but if she is, she will explain that in order to make a profit she must pay somewhat less than the appraised value. She may also first suggest that you may want to keep it in the family (if it has family history) or offer it for sale yourself.

Our examples are a little extreme, but we can't emphasize strongly enough the value of getting a good professional appraisal. If for any reason you feel that the appraisal may not be accurate, seek another. A second opinion is always worthwhile.

Dealers, Appraisers and Restorers

The following list of sources for buying and selling antique and collectible teddy bears is merely intended as a starting point, and is by no means comprehensive. Most of the sources listed here were provided to us; we are not personally familiar with all of them. You may find other sources close to your own area. We have used the following codes to indicate which services are offered by each source.

B/S: Buy & sell old bears

A: Appraisals

R: Repair & restoration

UNITED STATES

CALIFORNIA

Dolls & Bears of Charlton Court ....**B/S A R**
144 Marina Drive
Long Beach, CA 90803
Phone/FAX (562) 430-6443
Email: Charltonct.com

Dreamland Toys ....**B/S**
301 East Arrow Hwy.
Suite 106
San Dimas, CA 91773
(909) 305-1075
FAX: (909) 305-1987

Pat Johnson ....**R**
2335 Tulip Court
McKinleyville, CA 95519

Linda Mullins ....**B/S A**
P.O. Box 2327
Carlsbad, CA 92018
(760) 434-7444
FAX: 760-434-0154

John Paul Port ....**B/S A**
61 Laguna Drive
La Honda, CA 94020
(605) 747-0359
FAX: (605) 747-9725
Email: John@teddytoday.com
Web page: www.teddytoday.com

Rare Bears ....**B/S A R**
17831 Chase St.
Northridge, CA 91325
(818) 993-9361
FAX: (818) 993-9316
Email: rarebears@earthlink.com
Web page: www.rarebears.com

COLORADO

E. Adorjan ....**B/S A R**
P.O. Box 40601
Denver, CO 80204
(303) 761-7234
Email: Toyrep.com
Web page: members.aol.com/toyrep

DELAWARE

Loved to Pieces Doll Hospital ....**R**
105 Culver Drive
Laurel, DE 19956
(302) 875-4851

FLORIDA

Justa Kidigan Doll & Teddy Hospital ....**R**
380 Dumont Ave.
Deltona, FL 32738
(407) 302-6118
FAX: (407) 302-3323
Email: jkdollhosp@aol.com
Web site: www.webdolls.com/fl/jkhosp

Old-Timers' Antiques ....B/S
3717-B South Dixie Hwy.
West Palm Beach, FL 33405
Phone/FAX: (561) 832-5141
Email: Oldtimers2@aol.com
Web site: members.aol.com/
    oldtimers2/index.htm

PG's Enchanted Dolls &
The Doll Hospital ....R
4360 W. Oakland Pk. Blvd.
Ft. Lauderdale, FL 33313
(954) 739-9030
FAX: (954) 714-9597
Email: pgsdolls.com
Web site: www.pgsdolls.com/hospital. htm

MARYLAND

The Calico Teddy ....B/S A
22 East 24th St.
Baltimore, MD 21218
(410) 366-7011
FAX: (410) 889-4722
Email: caliceddy@aol.com
Web site: www.calicoteddy.com

D.L. Harrison Co. ....B/S A R
303 Deep Dale Court
Timonium, MD 21093
(410) 252-5192
FAX: (410) 252-5038

Old Friends Antiques ....B/S
P.O. Box 754
Sparks, MD 21152
Phone/FAX: (412) 291-1024
Email: petsybar@aol.com

Tim Stirn..R
6605 Johnnycake Rd.
Baltimore, MD 21244-2401
(410) 747-2368

Mort & Evelyn Wood ....B/S A R
505 Forest Lane
Towson, MD 21286
(410) 821-8960
Email: mortwood@home.com

MICHIGAN

Terry & Doris Michaud.......................................B/S
505 W. Broad St.
Chesaning, MI 48616
(517) 845-7881
FAX: (517) 845-6650
Email: dmmich217@aol.com

MINNESOTA

Antie Clare's Doll Hospital....................................R
2543 Seppala Blvd.
North St. Paul, MN 55109
(651) 770-7522
Web page: www.antieclares.com

NEW YORK

New York Doll Hospital ....R
787 Lexington Ave.
New York, NY 10021
(212) 838-7527

OHIO

Beck's Bears ....B/S R
P.O. Box 12755
Columbus, OH 43212
(614) 486-3238

Hanna Bruce Bears & Teddy Hospital ....R
4982 E. 88th St.
Garfield Heights, OH 44125
(216) 533-4082
Email: Hanna Bruce Bears@bigfoot.com
Web page: www.hannabrucebears.com

OREGON

Marge Adolphson..R
1327 SW Coast Ave.
Lincoln City, OR 97367
(503) 994-8497

Bunker Hill Bears..R
1820 Hamlet Court S.
Salem, OR 97302-3608
(503) 378-7705
Email: Leegent@open.org

Pat Niccolai ....**B/S A**
2434 15th Ave.
Forest Grove, OR 97116
(503) 359-9239
Email: pat_niccolai@yahoo.com

PENNSYLVANIA

Bears 'n Things ....**B/S A**
82 Timber Villa
Elizabethtown, PA 17022
(717) 367-4142
FAX: (717) 367-4143
Email: teddiesone@aol.com
Web page: www.deelor.com

The Country Bear ....**B/S A R**
251 Keswick Ave.
Glenside, PA 19038
Phone/FAX: (215) 576-8466
Email: jaysbears@aol.com
Web page: www.countrybear1.com

Harper General Store ....**B/S A**
RD#2 Box 512
Annville, PA 17003
(717) 865-3456
FAX: (717) 865-3813

TEXAS

Bear Corner ....**B/S A R**
Olde English Village
225-B East Amherst
Tyler, TX 7570l
(903) 534-1329
Email: bob boy71@aol.com

Bears by Janie ....R
208 Trailwood Drive
Euless, TX 76039
(817) 545-4462

B.C. & Co. Heirlooms...R
500-G N. Hwy. 377
Roanoke, TX 76262
(800) 290-0959

Pat Schlau Doll Workshop ....R
107 Dallas St.
P.O. Box 542
Winona, TX 75792
(903) 877-2420

VIRGINIA

Mar-Ke Mohair ....R
14440 Aldengate Rd.
Midlothian, VA 23113
(804) 794-3900
Email: marke@teddybearrepair.com
Web page: www.teddybearrepair.com

B/S: Buy & sell old bears • **A**: Appraisals • **R**: Repair & restoration

AUCTION HOUSES

All of the following auctioneers include teddy bears in their antique toy and doll auctions. Some offer specialty antique teddy bear sales. Contact them to be put on their mailing lists for announcement of upcoming sales. Many of these firms have also added on-line auctions to their schedules. For the most part, we have listed only the main office of an auction house. Some of these auctioneers are in more than one location, so be sure to ask for a list of all their branches.

Bill Bertoia Auctions
1881-T Spring Rd.
Vineland, NJ 08361
(856) 692-8697

Bonhams
Montpelier Street
London SW7 1HH
England
011 44 171-393-3900
FAX: 011 44 171-393-3905
Web site: www.bonhams.com

Butterfield Chicago
441 West Huron
Chicago, IL 60610
(312) 377-7500
FAX: (312) 377-7501

Christie's
20 Rockefeller Plaza
New York, New York 10020
(212) 636-2000
FAX: (212) 636-2399
Web site: www.christies.com

Christie's South Kensington
85 Old Brompton Road
London SW7 3LD
England UK
011 44 171-581-7611
FAX: 011 44 171-321-3321

Frashers
P.O. Box 142
Oak Grove, MO 64075
(816) 625-3786
FAX: (816) 625-6079

Hake's Americana & Collectibles
P. O. Box 1444
York, PA 17405
(717) 848-1333
FAX: (717) 852-0344

McMasters
5855 Glenn Highway
P.O. Box 1755
Cambridge, OH 43725
(740) 432-4320
FAX: (740) 432-3191

Richard Opfer Auctioneering Inc.
1919 Greenspring Drive
Timonium, MD 21093
(410) 252-5035

Phillips New York
406 East 79th ST.
New York, NY 10021
(212) 570-4830
FAX: (212) 570-2207

Skinner
357 Main St.
Bolton, MA 01740
(508) 779-6241
FAX: (508) 779-5144

Sotheby's New York
1334 York Ave.
New York, NY 10021
(212) 606-7000
FAX: (212) 606-7937
Web site: www.sothebys.com

Sotheby's London
34-35 New Bond St.
London W1A 2AA
England
011 44 171 293-5000
FAX: 011 44 293-5989

Theriault's
P.O. Box 151
Annapolis, MD 21404
(410) 224-3655
FAX: (410) 224-2515
Web site: www.theriaults.com

Toy Auction Barcelona
Figueras & Kaul S.L.
Apartado de Correos 6992
E-08080 Barcelona
Spain

INDEX

(by maker's name)

ABOUT THE AUTHORS

Terry and Doris Michaud are internationally recognized pioneers in the field of teddy bear collecting. They started their collection in the mid 1970s, when there was little demand for teddies, and it was not uncommon to buy a very early bear in top condition for as little as $100.

At the time the Michauds were dealing in antique dolls and toys, and a doll collector mentioned that she would like an old teddy. They soon found a forlorn bear with one ear missing, priced at $15. As the Michauds also operated a doll hospital, Doris was able to repair the bear and outfit it with a knitted sweater and a pair of wire-rimmed glasses. The Michauds' daughter Kim's comment that he looked like her music teacher inspired the name of "The Professor," which has stuck to this day.

The Michauds originally intended to sell this bear, but decided instead to display him at shows, holding a sign that read: "Wanted — old teddy bears." With The Professor's help, their collection grew rapidly and the day of actually selling a bear was put off for nearly 25 years.

Collecting bears eventually led to making bears that resembled the antiques they had taken to heart. One of their very first prototypes accompanied them on a 25th-wedding-anniversary trip to England where they met the late Peter Bull, the British actor whose books on teddy bears played a large role in building the growing interest in bear collecting. Bull encouraged the Michauds to market their bear. A second sample was shipped off to a dealer in Boston and a prompt return order launched the Carrousel line of teddy bears.

Within a few years the Michauds and several home workers were supplying more than 100 shops in 40 states and three foreign countries. Further expansion during the 1980s brought about the temporary production of their designs by the Dean's Company in England and distribution by Tide-Rider Inc. of California.

The Michauds have slowed their pace in recent years, and now craft a small number of teddies for a limited clientele, including the annual Walt Disney World Teddy Bear and Doll Convention, at which they have been featured guests since its inception. Frequently called on to be keynote speakers, they have shared their expertise with collectors as far afield as Brisbane, Australia. Authors of four books (*Bears Repeating*, 1985; *How to Make & Sell Quality Teddy Bears*, 1986; *Teddy Tales*, 1989; and *Contemporary Teddy Bear Price Guide*, 1992) they also write for magazines here and abroad. Their bear-making seminars are popular throughout the country, as are their classes in Chesaning, Michigan. With partners Bill and Rosemary Hayes, they operate the Keystone Traders annual British Teddy Tour.

In addition, the Michauds work with law enforcement agencies and the court system to provide expert witness testimony in cases involving teddy bears. They have appeared on TV shows throughout the country, including a teddy bear program that aired in December 1999 on the Discovery Channel.